WITNESS TO NORTH KOREA

ASIAN ARGUMENTS

Asian Arguments is a series of books which explores life in Asia today. Written by experts from the fields of journalism, academia and politics, all of whom have considerable experience of living and working in Asia, the books reveal how citizens across the region – from China to Vietnam – are confronting problems such as environmental crisis, economic development and democracy.

Available now in the series:

The Trouble with Taiwan by Kerry Brown and Kally Wu Tzu Hui
China and the New Maoists by Kerry Brown and Simone van Nieuwenhuizen
Leftover Women: The Resurgence of Gender Inequality in China by Leta Hong Fincher
North Korea by Paul French
A Kingdom in Crisis: Thailand's Struggle for Democracy in the Twenty-First Century by Andrew MacGregor Marshall
China's Urban Billion by Tom Miller
Ghost Cities of China by Wade Shepard
Return of the Junta: Why Myanmar's Military Must Go Back to the Barracks by Oliver Slow
Myanmar's Enemy Within: Buddhist Violence and the Making of a Muslim 'Other' by Francis Wade
Thailand: Shifting Ground between the US and a Rising China by Benjamin Zawacki
The Southern Tour: Deng Xiaoping and the Fight for China's Future by Jonathan Chatwin

WITNESS TO NORTH KOREA

Three Years on the Ground in the DPRK

Jerome Sauvage

BLOOMSBURY ACADEMIC
LONDON • NEW YORK • OXFORD • NEW DELHI • SYDNEY

BLOOMSBURY ACADEMIC
Bloomsbury Publishing Plc, 50 Bedford Square, London, WC1B 3DP, UK
Bloomsbury Publishing Inc, 1359 Broadway, New York, NY 10018, USA
Bloomsbury Publishing Ireland, 29 Earlsfort Terrace, Dublin 2, D02 AY28, Ireland

BLOOMSBURY, BLOOMSBURY ACADEMIC and the Diana logo are trademarks of Bloomsbury Publishing Plc

First published in Great Britain 2026

Cover illustration: North Korean (DPRK) propaganda poster glorifying agricultural production, *c*. 1950s © Alamy.com
Cover design Francis Kenney

A catalogue record for this book is available from the British Library.

Library of Congress Cataloging-in-Publication Data

ISBN: HB: 978-1-3505-6844-0
PB: 978-1-3505-6842-6
ePDF: 978-1-3505-6846-4
eBook: 978-1-3505-6845-7

Series: Asian Arguments

Typeset by RefineCatch Limited, Bungay, Suffolk
Printed and bound in Great Britain

For product safety related questions contact productsafety@bloomsbury.com.

To the memory of Gilbert, my father, and Wing, my father-in-law,
who believed in the value of cooperation among people and nations,
and to the people of North Korea

* * *

Authorization kills conscience. As for dictators, the only mystery there is that they've awarded themselves authorization. They don't just want to numb conscience, they want to kill it off. And they've done so!

Joseph Roth, *Die Zukunft* (Paris, 1938)

When people call you a veteran North Korea-watcher, it merely means you've had more time to be more wrong in more ways.

Aidan Foster-Carter
Senior Research Fellow and veteran NK-watcher, Leeds University

CONTENTS

ILLUSTRATIONS

Figures

Table

PREFACE

I served as United Nations Resident Coordinator and Resident Representative for the United Nations Development Programme (UNDP) in the Democratic People's Republic of Korea (DPRK) from November 2009 until early 2013, three years that were at once professionally intense and deeply personal. This memoir is a record of what I saw, tried to do and what I still carry forward.

During the time that my wife Carolyn and I spent in the DPRK , we witnessed two moments of acute inter-Korean tension, the death of Kim Jong Il and the subsequent leadership transition to the third generation of the Kim family, and the continued development of the country's nuclear programme amid profound economic hardship.

I reopened the UNDP office which had been closed under heavy pressure from the US Government, recruited a team of expatriate and national Korean staff and launched new programme initiatives. As UN Coordinator, I supported the United Nations Agencies as they delivered essential humanitarian aid to the population, observed the first census in fifteen years and ensured coordinated responses to two natural disasters. I left the country with new programmes underway and many relationships intact. This memoir recounts that experience, as I remember now.

It took a decade for me to begin writing this account. After the DPRK, I was assigned to Washington, DC, with UNDP, and then I retired from the UN. I accepted a few post-retirement consultancies in Yemen and other places, which capped off a fulfilling career that included UNDP postings (with my family in tow) in Vietnam, Cambodia, New York City, Madagascar, India and Pakistan.

Yet North Korea lingered. The country, its people and its future stayed with me – unfinished business of a kind. Always an avid reader of novels in French and English, I explored fiction writing, perhaps to create distance from past events or because I was hesitant to write about myself, or perhaps because fiction is the only approach to this enigmatic country. I took classes on English and American literature, joined writing classes and groups in New York. But it was quickly apparent that I was not suited to write the next great novel.

It then dawned on me that I was regularly asked to speak about the DPRK on a broad range of topics – humanitarian issues, expatriate life on the inside, the nitty-gritty of development work in the DPRK – and had accumulated a trove of notes, presentations and writings. These could form the basis for a different kind of story. A few trusted colleagues and friends encouraged me to write my own account.

I found how difficult it is to write about my experience in North Korea. The environment in which we worked was not transparent, sometimes quite the opposite. Information of all kinds, even the most banal sort, was sensitive, often hidden. The North Koreans had to remain careful to avoid proximity to foreigners, past and present, as it might affect them or their families. The international personnel who worked with the DPRK often preferred to stay out of the spotlight. With the exception of publicly known officials at the UN and in various governments, and of Mr Zharas Takenov who contributed to this book, the names of all the North Korean individuals and expatriates have been changed, and are sometimes with only a first name. Conversations are not offered as verbatim quotations: they are reconstructed from memory and notes. I have aimed within such constraints to present truthfully and accurately my stories, reflections of what I personally saw and heard.

When the Covid-19 pandemic closed the borders of the DPRK in 2020, the writing project took on a new sense of urgency. Now in mid-2026, six years have passed since all expatriates departed the country when the DPRK sealed its borders. A few embassies have recently reopened in Pyongyang but to my knowledge neither the UN Country Team, international NGOs nor bilateral aid agencies have returned.

Two years ago, a group of North Korea experts published a paper reflecting on three decades of international engagement with the DPRK, aiming to guide future efforts once the country reopens.[1] In that spirit, I see this memoir as a dispatch from the field, a description of what we tried to accomplish and how we went about it. And while details on the ground will have shifted, the core realities described will, I believe, likely endure. I hope the book may serve researchers, policy-makers, humanitarian professionals and the curious public – who may one day engage with the DPRK, a singular place.

ACKNOWLEDGEMENTS

Many contributors to this book will remain unnamed for the understandable reason that association with such a publication may not facilitate their professional engagement with the DPRK. Several of these individuals are still expecting to travel to the DPRK – now or in the future. They will recognize their input, though any errors or interpretative differences are solely my responsibility. I can however name some to whom I owe a particular debt of gratitude in the preparation of this book: Geraldine Pelletier and Jamie Banfill, who reviewed many chapters, Julie Brossy, Ambassador John Everard and Professor Hazel Smith at the School of Oriental and African Studies, University of London. These friends and colleagues have encouraged and supported me from the very beginning of this project.

I am grateful to my UN and NGO colleagues and friends, both North Korean and foreigners, in the DPRK and elsewhere and especially my UNDP colleagues. Although their names are not included to maintain confidentiality and protect their ongoing professional activities, they are present throughout this book. I have and continue to depend on their insights, comradeship and support. Others, outside of the DPRK, have been absolutely crucial to shaping my experiences in North Korea: at the UN, Ted Martell, Selva Ramachandran, Jon Brause and Vongvieng Saensathit. And more recently, Jean Lee, Jenny Town and the members and staff at the National Committee on North Korea (NCNK) in Washington DC, with Keith Luse, NK News with Chad O'Carroll and HanVoice with Sean Chung.

Respect goes to the people of North Korea whom I met in and outside of Pyongyang, on farms, in hospitals and in their homes, who experience daily lives under unremitting pressure and yet manage to get up every morning and try and live and to those with the courage to advance an openness agenda within the regime.

While much of this book is based on my own observations, I also relied on many scholars and North Korea experts, acknowledged in the Notes and Bibliography. Any omissions are unintentional.

I learned much from Series Editor Paul French and from David Avital at Zed Books in London, who first enthusiastically took up this project and patiently stewarded this manuscript to completion. And then there are the many North Koreans who will hopefully get the chance to make their country a better place. I hope one day to be able to thank them by name.

And most importantly, I am grateful to my children Matthieu and Claire and their wonderful families for their support and to my wife Carolyn, who contributed extensively to the project and without whom none of this would ever have happened.

NOTE ON SPELLING

North Korean names: I have chosen to use the North Korean way of writing names with the surname first, followed by the given name, with each word capitalized and no hyphens used. For example, the name of Kim Jong Un will be written with no hyphens.

ABBREVIATIONS

Abbreviations

CEDAW	Convention for the Elimination of All Forms of Discrimination Against Women
COMECON	Council for Mutual Economic Assistance
CRPD	Convention on the Rights of Persons with Disabilities
DMZ	Demilitarized Zone
DPRK	Democratic People's Republic of Korea
FTB	Foreign Trade Bank
GSB	General Service Bureau
IFTJ	International Finance and Trade Joint Company
MFA	Ministry of Foreign Affairs
NCNK	National Committee on North Korea
NGO	non-governmental organization
OECD	Organisation for Economic Cooperation and Development
PDC	Public Distribution Centre
PIWA	Pyongyang International Women's Group
SAIS	Johns Hopkins' School of Advanced International Studies
TB	tuberculosis
UN	United Nations
UNCT	United Nations Country Team
UNDP	United Nations Development Programme
UNFPA	United Nations Population Fund
UNICEF	United Nations Children's Fund
UNIDO	United Nations Industrial Development Organization
UNTAC	United Nations Transitional Authority in Cambodia
WHO	World Health Organization
WFP	World Food Programme
WPK	Workers' Party of Korea

Part I

ARRIVAL AND COLLISION

Chapter 1

CALL TO NORTH KOREA

Arrival in Pyongyang – Looking back at UNDP's North Korea 'scandal' – Doubts about the UN, and my career – Our expertise in Asian Communist dictatorships

I wanted to think that the United Nations 'tethered' the Democratic People's Republic of Korea (DPRK) to the rest of the world, until a friend told me that the country appeared fundamentally untethered. I settled with the word 'connected'. The UN is a key link between North Korea and the global community. The World Health Organization (WHO), United Nations Children's Fund (UNICEF) and the Global Fund participate in the global war on tuberculosis (TB) and establish and enforce international health standards; the International Civil Aviation Organization certifies commercial aircraft; United Nations Industrial Development Organization (UNIDO) recycles Soviet-era electric capacitators in an environmentally acceptable manner; UNESCO sees to it that Koguryo Tombs meet World Heritage requirements,[1] and the year I arrived in North Korea, United Nations Population Fund (UNFPA) delivered a successful population census, that met international standards.

In the DPRK, foreign embassies, UN agencies and international NGOs interact with the government through tightly controlled and hierarchical channels, with the Ministry of Foreign Affairs (MFA) serving as the primary point of contact. UN agencies and NGOs working on humanitarian or development programmes are typically required to coordinate with both the MFA and sector-specific ministries, with project approval and access permissions subject to multilayered scrutiny. Inside the MFA, there is a bureau for relations with US organizations, one for the Europeans, one for the UN and so on. And then there is the General Service Bureau (GSB): landlord, rent and tax collector, facilities manager, utility provider and surveillance coordinator.

* * *

I awoke jet-lagged, crumpled in my seat, next to a man standing in the aisle. He picked up a red badge from a small jewel box and pinned it on his jacket lapel, carefully, above his heart. I watched him fasten the red badge with the careful precision one reserves for sacred rituals. It was muscle memory, a gesture performed countless times before. To me, it felt like an initiation into a world I had only read about and was now preparing to enter.

'We're approaching Pyongyang Airport,' Carolyn said. She looked more alert than I felt, after our long flight from New York, a stopover in Beijing and finally this trip aboard Air Koryo, the North Korean airline.

Outside my window, pale golden rays covered bare fields, deserted dirt roads and a few roofs of corrugated metal whose gleam was long gone. It was the end of autumn. The whole perimeter around the airport seemed uninhabited, like around a military base. Our Tupolev Tu-204 landed and taxied for an unusually long time on the runway, deserted except for a single MiG fighter jet, a red star on its fuselage, ready to scramble.

The airport's single building was nothing more than a one-story hangar. Perched on the roof was a huge portrait of Kim Il Sung, the father-founder of the DPRK, who smiled jovially, as if he'd just thought of a great joke for all his people to hear. A little intimidated, I paused atop the stair ladder above the tarmac and took in the cold air. All around us were electrified fences and barren hills. After the drone of the aircraft, I expected noise, movement – some sign of life. Instead, the only sound was the wind brushing against the barren hills. Above our heads, migratory birds flew southward in formation. They would soon cross over the Demilitarized Zone (DMZ) to enter South Korea. Uniformed army officers pointed the passengers to a bus waiting at the foot of the ladder. I turned toward the cabin. Did I want to forget the whole thing and return to a normal place? Yes, I might have. But the crew was already preparing to disembark. There was no going back. UN rules said that for a 'hardship posting' such as this one, staff were assigned for at least two years, and the Representative for an additional year. The tour of duty we had signed up for, began now.

The passport officer stamped my UN laissez-passer, a diplomatic travel document from the UN. Some countries accept it, but others, like the USA, do not. In North Korea, I viewed it as a potential safeguard from my international organization. The officer was a young woman wearing red lipstick, high-heeled shoes and a huge Soviet-era green cap. I was almost disappointed at how little interest she showed Carolyn's US passport. As per procedures with Americans, the officer stamped the visa on a loose leaf so it would not remain inside her regular passport whenever she needed to return home.

Behind the officer, North Korean soldiers grabbed bundles from the creaky conveyor belt and quickly took them away. When our luggage arrived, a young man came forward to meet us.

'*Annyeong ha simika*,' he said in greeting, and directed us to a security check with a portal, where military personnel opened our luggage.

'Why are they taking my iPhone,' I asked?

'You get your phone back when you exit the country.'

Whereas in 2009 we were not as dependent on smartphones as today, parting from it made me feel cold and exposed, like waiting alone in a hospital gown. Ironically, North Korea eventually allowed foreigners to bring their mobile phones into the country the month that I definitively departed. The young man ushered us into a room by the side of the building. In the lounge, thick carpets muffled all sounds. High on the wall, portraits of Kim Il Sung and Kim Jong Il, the father-and-son rulers, watched us sternly. A mirror stood from floor to ceiling, and when I got near it, I thought I detected movement inside the mirror – either it was two-way or paranoia got the better of me. I felt more disoriented than usual. Was it jet lag? After a short wait, a middle-aged man entered the room and said in precise English that his name was Song Ho So from the MFA.

Mr. Song was slightly shorter than me, wore a well-cut black suit with a black tie with gold stripes, black shoes and a thick, well-tailored wool coat. There was a red pin on the lapel. In my years working with him, I never saw him dress differently, except for the regulation short-sleeved shirt in summer. His black hair was thinning, his glasses were gold-rimmed and his small hands were manicured. Over the next few years, it became clear that Mr Song and I didn't care much for each other. Song became a nemesis of sort for me, and I, his permanent disappointment. Thankfully, others among the MFA team proved to be more collaborative counterparts.

We followed Song to a black car parked by the curb. It was a 6-cylinder Audi, fast and sleek. The interior was elegant and roomy, even luxurious. 'This is the UNDP [United Nations Development Programme] Representative's car,' Song said. What was such a car doing in North Korea? I would have expected to see it on a German autobahn and that in Pyongyang I'd be given a more rugged car as was normal from previous postings. This purchase was unusual for my Agency and felt inappropriate. A Rep's car should indicate 'field-readiness', some attempt at modesty.

A light, wiry man was leaning against the Audi, smoking a cigarette. His face was deeply marked. 'My name is Pak. I am your driver,' he said in decent English. His narrow smile was guarded but friendly. Was he startled that Carolyn was ethnically Chinese, or had he been briefed in advance? Either way, he didn't show it. Although he and I clocked many hours together in the Audi, I never knew what Pak really thought. Inside the car, he heard everything I said, and perhaps – no, certainly – reported it all to his real bosses. And yet Pak also provided a kind of protection over me, and once astonished me when, on a project visit, he quietly told off a district officer who had a little too much to drink. The man immediately ceased annoying me. After that, I always wondered about Mr Pak's status in the regime, *exactly*. Over our three years together, we shared a few presents, cigarettes and lots of ping-pong games, and I mourned his parents' passing, to the extent I was allowed.

We stopped in front of the car. Unsure of myself, I hesitated. Should we take the back seat or the front seat? Was this Mr Song's way of asserting dominance from the start? Carolyn caught my eye, amused at my overthinking. In the end, I decided that I should follow some kind of protocol. Carolyn and I slid into the backseat.

* * *

The drive to Pyongyang felt like a 1950s documentary about Mao's China: green army trucks ferried people, standing or crouching and holding onto their caps. A troop of boys and girls marched along the road wearing red scarves. They were probably singing in unison, but our windows were closed against the cold and I couldn't hear them. A few riders dressed in padded green vests and canvas pants, passed by on old bicycles, though far fewer than in Maoist China. But the year was 2009, and the environment looked so different from the bustling, modern China we had just left, with its market economy, its speedy cars and shiny buildings. From the silence in the car, I watched grey apartment blocks sitting amid the fields, window frames blackened by soot like dirty domino tiles dropped from above. A few women stooped to collect something on the ground, perhaps kernels of corn or wheat left from recent harvests and held them in one hand like a beggar's cup upturned toward the sky. It was the end of the day, the light declined and the landscape seemed colder still. This time capsule playing in silent mode increased my sense of disconnect.

Our car entered Pyongyang, North Korea's showcase capital city. With high-rise towers of glass and steel, downtown had some of the visual trappings of any Asian city's modern business districts, minus the traffic. Along wide avenues, a few pedestrians and bicyclists shared the road with a scatter of cars.

I have always thought that you can sense the spirit of a city within the first hours of arriving in it. These first impressions soon dilute into a sort of familiarity, just as we stop noticing the features of a person who at first vividly impresses us. Some cities display their personality in the street, in full view: everyday life effortlessly exposes itself to the visitor, from goods displayed in shop windows to patrons sitting unguarded on café terraces. Passers-by loiter, meet and chat in plain view. Other cities reveal themselves more reluctantly because so much of life happens 'on the inside': a window that reveals a face through curtains for a brief instant, a shaded bazaar inviting coolness and protection from the sun, or a warm, inviting brightly lit brasserie where friends take refuge from the winter cold.

But in downtown Pyongyang that late afternoon, life was to be found neither inside nor outside. There was no visible business conducted on the streets, shops seemed empty of customers and windows revealed no signs of life inside apartments. The architecture was cohesive, polished, without curves or the odd additions that time tolerates, like a balcony or an awning. Everything was flat, guarded – flat surfaces, smooth glass windows on the ground floor, guarded expressions on faces. Downtown Pyongyang felt like the empty showcase of a mid-century department store. Where did everyday life really take place? To find out what life in North Korea looked like, I began to think we would have to start searching behind those façades.

Song informed us that the UNDP complex, comprising the office and our apartment, needed renovation, so we would spend a few days in a hotel. The car stopped in front of a building covered in orange stucco with shades of pink called the Pothonggang Hotel. The hotel was a nine-story modern building, centrally located along the Pothonggang River, which reminded me of the 1970s Moscow Intourist hotels: lots of marble, wide corridors, and the absence of guests gave it a solemn but slightly haunted atmosphere. It was very clean, with shiny, polished floors. We learned that it was one of the few places where you could watch foreign news such as the BBC and, sometimes, CNN. The rooms were comfortable enough, with a kettle and a cup and saucer, an empty bar fridge and a wall calendar.

We set our luggage down and prepared for our first night in Pyongyang. Once in bed, before falling asleep, I reviewed the career trajectory that got me there.

* * *

The year was 2008. I was reaching the end of a four-year assignment managing Operations for UNDP in India. I had started to wonder: was the UN making any sort of difference, or just coasting on autopilot? Too many meetings that danced around real issues, too many reports never acted upon. In a complex country like India, I felt that UNDP's programmes were simply too small to effectively address the problems of an immense population and major economy. The Government of India had the capacity and resources to take challenges on its own. Professionally, I was ready to take on an assignment where the UN was really needed and could make a meaningful difference – if only I could find the right one. Seeing that I would need some time to sort myself out, Carolyn wisely decided to resume her own career as a non-profit consultant in New York City. And now, North Korea had come calling. I was to reopen the UNDP office and assume the position of UN Coordinator.

* * *

Through our travels and assignments, Carolyn and I became students of sorts of twentieth-century Asian communism. We met at the Johns Hopkins' School of Advanced International Studies (SAIS) in Washington, DC. I had studied French Administrative Law in Paris and completed my then-mandatory military service. Although fewer French citizens than today left the country to study and work, I chose to go to the United States. From a young age, I only imagined my life overseas. In Washington, DC, where I studied US Foreign Policy at Johns Hopkins' SAIS, Ronald Reagan had just been elected. Though many already foresaw the end of the Soviet Union, I still studied the Cold War and its aftermath, including strategic defence systems, intercontinental ballistic missiles and mutual assured destruction, as if it remained the dominant reality in world affairs. After graduation, I applied to international jobs and obtained a two-year junior associate post with the UNDP who sent me to Vietnam.

Carolyn attended Antioch College in the United States in the late 1970s when, barely twenty years old, she first visited China, joining an early cohort of young American students who travelled to the People's Republic in the wake of Nixon's historic visit in 1972. Afterwards, she lived and worked in Beijing and Taiwan on and off for a few years and learned rudimentary Chinese. As a Chinese-American born in California, this did represent a return to her roots but her interests extended beyond China alone and she chose to study international development and politics.

Carolyn and I married and travelled to Hanoi. Eight years after the end of the fall of Saigon, she was one of the very few Americans allowed to visit or live in Vietnam. But I took it as a positive sign when the official at the Vietnamese Embassy in Bangkok stepped out of his office to hand me her visa and, smiling from cheek to cheek, vigorously shook my hand.

In 1983, Vietnam was still part of the Council for Mutual Economic Assistance (COMECON), the economic agreement tying communist nations to the Soviet Union. The UN represented then an ostensibly neutral organization between East and West, able to deliver Western technologies. There was much to do: the country was devastated from decades of struggle: years of conflict and decolonization from France, the war with the United States and, in 1979, a short but intense military confrontation with China following Vietnam's ouster of the Khmer Rouge regime and Cambodia's subsequent occupation. The UNDP assigned to me a nationwide reconstruction project that suffered from oversized ambitions, communist bureaucracy, and an initial lack of trust between us and the government. In the end, it was precisely trust that got us through our difficulties and on the way to good projects. Although the UN had operated only in the South during the war, we eventually convinced the Northerners that we respected a united Vietnam's right to sovereignty and to make its own choices. By the time the country began to interact with large development banks and private Western investors, UNDP (and other UN organizations) had become dependable, impartial advisors. This successful precedent no doubt led me to apply to – and to be considered as a candidate for – the North Korea assignment.

After Hanoi, we visited China in the 1980s and kept in touch with both Vietnamese and Chinese friends and family and witnessed the positive impact of reforms implemented by Deng Xiaoping's Four Modernizations and Vietnam's own economic reform process called *Doi Moi*. These two economic reforms were governed by the need to bring a measure of individual initiative to economic activity and liberalism to society and to open these two countries to the outside world, facilitating technology transfer and trade. When these reforms took place in these two countries, millions of people's lives improved.

Some facets of our lives and work proved to be apt preparation for the DPRK. For example, both the Vietnamese and the Chinese, at the time, closely controlled everyone's lives and discouraged contacts between locals and foreigners, albeit not as strictly as we discovered to be the case in North Korea. Also, the administration – and the competitive sharing – of power within the respective regimes offered evident similarities with the DPRK, such as the competitive co-existence of a Party, a military apparatus and a government inside the communist regimes.

The optimism behind the reforms and consequent opening in China and Vietnam constituted additional reasons to want to work in the DPRK. In Hanoi, we became close with a young mother of two working at UNDP, who had lost two men in her life: her father, killed by the French and then her fiancé, to the Americans. Whilst we lived in Hanoi, she started a small business selling chicken and flowers. Within twenty years she was running a very successful chain of convenience stores throughout the Vietnamese capital, and we remain friends to this day.

In 1985 in Hanoi, we had met a young US Representative named John McCain, accompanied by American TV newsman Walter Cronkite. They had come to Vietnam on the ten-year anniversary of the Fall of Saigon. We all sat on the floor of a modest two-bedroom apartment in the expatriates' four-story building. McCain showed me his broken arm, which he could no longer flex, following his bomber plane crash in the heart of Hanoi. Carolyn was the only one who watched Walter Cronkite growing up and she was star-struck. He regaled us with stories of reporting from the Soviet Union. After this visit, McCain worked in the US Senate, for a rapprochement and exactly ten years after his visit, the US and Vietnam re-established diplomatic relations.

Having witnessed such momentous change in China and Vietnam, how could we not be hopeful that North Korea could follow a path towards change, comparable to other communist countries in the region? As we set foot for the first time in Pyongyang, how could we not hope to witness, even accompany, such possible, historic change?

When the North Koreans initially objected to my going with a US spouse, I answered that after our twenty-five years of marriage, I had no intention of going alone. I was pleasantly surprised when they accepted almost immediately. They must have eagerly awaited UNDP's return, I assumed.

* * *

The next day, our first morning in Pyongyang, we awoke to loudspeakers reverberating over the trees and the tall buildings. The voice of a woman penetrated the room – trembling, insistent and mournful, as if a great sorrow had affected the country. Then her narration exploded in exultant swagger with an overly lyrical accent reminding me of the voice of commentators in old newsreels. Her voice pursued me to every corner of the room as her monologue climaxed, then ended abruptly, leaving me with the same oppressive sensation of distance and incomprehension as I'd felt the day before. To Carolyn, it brought back memories of her university in Beijing, when she used to jokingly respond to the unasked-for exhortations and music with a capitalist threat to invest in better quality loudspeakers and make a fortune.

Through the window, I watched pedestrians and cyclists pass outside the perimeter of our hotel. I remembered from my briefing in New York that we could walk outside our hotel or housing through the streets of Pyongyang, but should not try to approach passers-by. I felt conflicted. How do you build trust in a country where everything – even a conversation – feels like a transaction? How do you understand a place that refuses to be understood? As I listened to the woman's refrains rise and fall over the loudspeaker, I realized that my real challenge here wasn't just reopening an office. It was figuring out whether anything we did would actually matter.

[illegible] over at the [illegible] ultimately [illegible] abruptly, leaving me with the same [illegible] sensation of distance and incomprehension [illegible] the day before. To Caro [illegible] brought back memories of [illegible] in Beijing, when she used to jokingly respond to [illegible] threat to [illegible] years [illegible]

[illegible] watching [illegible] passersby [illegible] the patterns of [illegible] [illegible] How do [illegible] that recalls [illegible] and had [illegible] wanted [illegible] opening [illegible] whether anything we did would actually matter.

Chapter 1.5

Before the Return: UNDP's North Korean Scandal

The 'UNDP–North Korea scandal', as Fox News called it,[1] rocked my agency to its core. The UNDP was (and still is) the UN's lead agency for international development. Its work focused on helping countries build enough capacity to address challenges such as poverty, climate change and democratic governance. The UNDP had acquired its identity supporting the post-Second World War colonial world's access to independence during the 1960s and retained from that period a foundational respect for countries' right to self-determination (over time, this commitment would sometimes overshadow any concern for the new countries' record on good governance or human rights). With country offices throughout the developing world, UNDP prided itself on a strategic flexibility to meet the ever-changing needs of the countries in which it was located.

The UNDP and the Government of North Korea first began cooperation in 1979 when the UNDP opened an office in Pyongyang.[2] The UNDP focused then on improving food production and economic and environmental management through transfer of knowledge and technology. During the 1990s, the focus shifted to humanitarian aid in response to the food crisis. After 2000, however, the programme returned to its original, UNDP-mandated development orientation. By the time the UNDP suspended its operations in 2007, development projects had included 26 agriculture projects, 38 policy and planning projects focused on development issues, 9 energy projects, 15 environmental projects and 6 trade and development projects. These combined the provision of technical assistance, training and some equipment including, sometimes, advanced Western technology.

It had been well known that the United States Government harboured concerns about the presence and extent of the UNDP programme in North Korea. Since 1994, federal law required the United States to decrease its contribution to UNDP by an amount equivalent to UNDP's total expenditures in North Korea. To implement this statutory requirement, Congressional practice had been to reduce the total amount of funds appropriated to UNDP by the percentage of UNDP spending in North Korea.[3] In 2002, President George W. Bush labelled North Korea in his first State of the Union Address as part of an 'Axis of Evil'. Yet the US Administration had no reason to force an end to the UNDP programme in the DPRK. That changed in 2006, when the 'UNDP–North Korea scandal' offered an opportunity to do so.[4] An Albanian whistle-blower working as a UNDP contractor in the DPRK alleged that accounting malpractice was taking place inside the North Korea office. After his contract was not renewed, he contacted Congresswoman Ros-Lehtinen, a Cuban American Republican from Florida with strong anti-communist sentiment, who was Ranking Member of the House Committee on Foreign Affairs. She investigated whether UNDP had engaged in retaliation against the whistle-blower. The case became a crisis when the Senator decided that UNDP was not forthright enough in its responses. UNDP had unsuccessfully tried to claim diplomatic immunity as an international organization. Whereas international law recognizes some diplomatic status to UN agencies including UNDP, diplomatic immunity in the UN does not equal that enjoyed by foreign embassies. In any case, there was no need to invoke immunity: the United States had initially asked for clarifications, not investigated a crime or suggested a violation of international law.

The case soon strained UN–US relations. The US Senate Permanent Subcommittee on Investigations, chaired by Senator Carl Levin, a Democrat and Chair of the Committee on Homeland Security and Governmental Affairs, initiated a full investigation. This was the first time a full US Congress investigation targeted a UN agency.[5]

Some US Senate Panel findings appeared serious, while others were anecdotal. The Panel revealed that the UNDP safe in Pyongyang held US$3,500 in counterfeit currency for ten years. A consultant had returned his fee, complaining that he had been paid in 'monkey money'. Not sure what to do with the money, the UNDP office kept it in the safe for a decade. Potentially more serious, like an international spy mystery, there were unexplained UNDP transfers through Macau. The Panel discovered that in 2002, North Korea made payments (US$2.72 million) to various DPRK diplomatic missions abroad through a bank account intended to be used solely for UNDP activities. The funds had been used as a conduit to a Chinese company known as the International Finance and Trade Joint Company (IFTJ). Each transaction had moved the funds from the UNDP bank account at the Foreign Trade Bank

(FTB) in Pyongyang to an IFTJ account at the Macau-based Banco Delta Asia, referencing UNDP in the wire transfer documents.

Some revelations looked concerning, such as the finding by the Panel that transfers for US$50,000 in the name of UNDP had gone to a company with ties to Zang Lok Trading Co. in Macau, which a US State Department official later identified as having 'ties to a North Korean entity that had been designated [by the US Government] as the main North Korean financial agent for sales of conventional arms, ballistic missiles, and goods related to the assembly and manufacture of such weapons'. These payments were made through UNDP on behalf of other non-resident UN Agencies in the DPRK.

In North Korea, UNDP conducted its financial transactions with the DPRK-owned FTB, the DPRK's primary international commercial bank. FTB accepted paperwork only from North Korean personnel, sometimes routed UNDP funds through an unrelated bank account, and had refused to provide UNDP with copies of cancelled checks.

In their defence, UNDP pointed out that whereas they had not been aware of these transfers, they had all taken place before 2003, that is to say, well before the US authorities flagged Banco Delta Asia as suspicious. Nor had UNDP management any way of knowing Zang Lok was connected to North Korean weapons sales.[6]

However valid UNDP's explanations, in the eyes of the US Administration and some major donors such as Japan, the damage was done. The US Senate wrote in its investigation report that the DPRK had 'moved money out of the DPRK in order to evade sanctions' and had 'executed deceptive financial transactions' with UNDP's unwitting knowledge.[7] Later on, in Pyongyang, a former Representative at another UN agency had told me later on that his office had been contacted to make such payments abroad and that he had flatly refused. He asked me, with 100% hindsight, why couldn't UNDP have done the same.

In the end, UNDP decided to go to the root causes of the issues and empowered their own investigation panel (2008)[8], whose report led to organization-wide reforms. But these actions came too late and UNDP could not counter the US Senate report's contention that it had allowed the DPRK Government to use its banking channels to contravene sanctions[9]. Within the organization, there would always be a 'before the North Korea case' and an 'after the case', when UNDP thoroughly revamped its internal procedures and controls.

Under pressure from the US and a few other donors, and still struggling to gather all the information needed to get to the bottom of the situation, the UNDP Board felt compelled to suspend operations in North Korea as of 1 March 2007.[10] The responsibility for UN Coordination was handed over to World Food Programme (WFP), the largest UN Agency in the DPRK.

This wide-ranging dispute between a UN Agency and the United States Government had been waiting to happen and UNDP was the perfect foil. A few years earlier, the then-UN Secretary-General Kofi Annan had angered the Bush Administration when he declared the 2003 invasion of Iraq illegal.[11] His Deputy, Sir Mark Malloch Brown, had successfully led UNDP through reforms and spectacular growth from 1999 to 2005. During the Bush administration, foreign policy hawk John Bolton's controversial two-year term as Ambassador to the UN further damaged the US-UN relationship. The traditional ties between UNDP and the US Government had loosened. When the North Korea scandal became public, the UNDP Administrator was a renowned Turkish economist, no particular friend to the Bush Administration. In 2007, the year of the UNDP North Korea case, a scandal in Iraq nicknamed Oil-for-Food, revealed widespread corruption and abuse at the UN, though UNDP was not implicated. To make things worse, on the Korean peninsula, ballistic missile launches and a nuclear test in 2006 resulted in UN Security Council sanctions and rising tensions with North Korea.

It was in the DNA of UNDP to be a global organization, with an effective presence in almost all programme countries. After almost three years, no one inside the Agency or within the UN General Assembly could imagine keeping the DPRK office closed for much longer. The problem was that the circumstances that had led to programme suspension had made the re-opening that much trickier: on the one hand, board members like the United States or Japan doubted our ability to maintain control over our operations in North Korea, while on the other hand, countries from the Global South resented what they perceived as the rich countries' heavy-handed intervention into UNDP's business. It was therefore decided that the new programme would focus on helping the most vulnerable people in North Korea, while reassuring members of the executive board that UNDP were not going to lose control again over its operations.

In 2009, the UNDP Executive Board[12] finally authorized UNDP to re-open the Pyongyang office under a new, very different control environment affecting all operational aspects. This was going to be a very different UNDP office. Our organization had recognized the influence that various key donor countries could have on its internal operations. I was not sure that the North Korean Government was fully aware of that changed context.

Chapter 2

DIFFICULT START

UNDP premises in bad shape – Doomed currency reform – Early pressure regarding old projects

North Korea's humanitarian situation suggests a state of crisis in many ways different from the rest of the world. Whereas indicators of malnutrition and maternal mortality place the DPRK in a comparable situation to countries gripped by famine or conflict, the emergency is not caused by a natural disaster or a civil war. North Korea's predicament is systemic, rooted in long-standing policies and chronic neglect. North Korea cannot import enough cereal and agriculture implements from abroad to compensate its prevalent food production deficit. As to the health system, under-investment dates back to at least the mid-1990s. For these reasons, the UN and other humanitarian actors describe the humanitarian situation in North Korea as a chronic emergency, also defined as a long-drawn-out humanitarian situation.

* * *

Our first few weeks in Pyongyang were full of surprises, some of which were not too pleasant. The first one was the poor state of the UNDP office and of our apartment, which had been left unoccupied and, as far as I could tell, neglected for three years. On the morning after our arrival, our driver, Mr Pak, met us at the hotel and drove us to our place of work and home. We slowed down in front of an open gate with two guards and a sign that read: 'Munsudong Diplomatic Area'. That was the zone where most diplomats and workers from UN and NGOs lived and worked. Munsudong was about a mile long, neat and stern, ordered, a little like the Officers' Quarter on a military base, lined with good-looking trees. We slowly followed a central street lined by individual buildings with plaques providing the names of embassies and international agencies, with an armed North Korean sentry standing outside each building. There was little foot traffic, although I did note that North Koreans pedestrians could and did walk through the area.

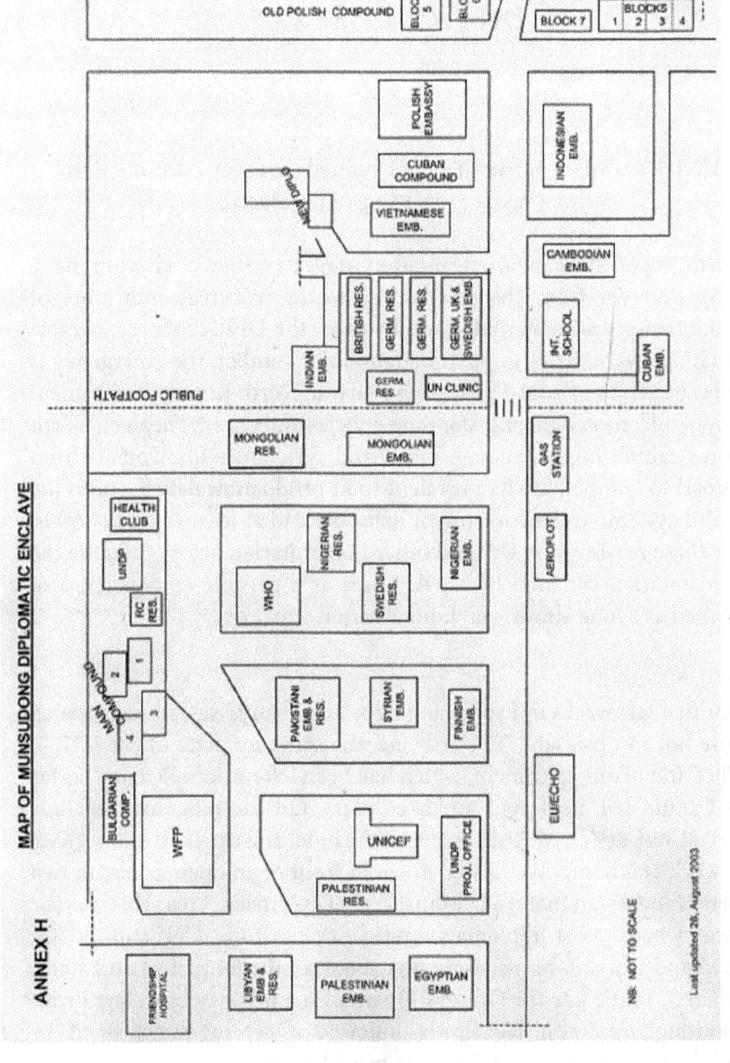

Map of Munsudong circa 2010.

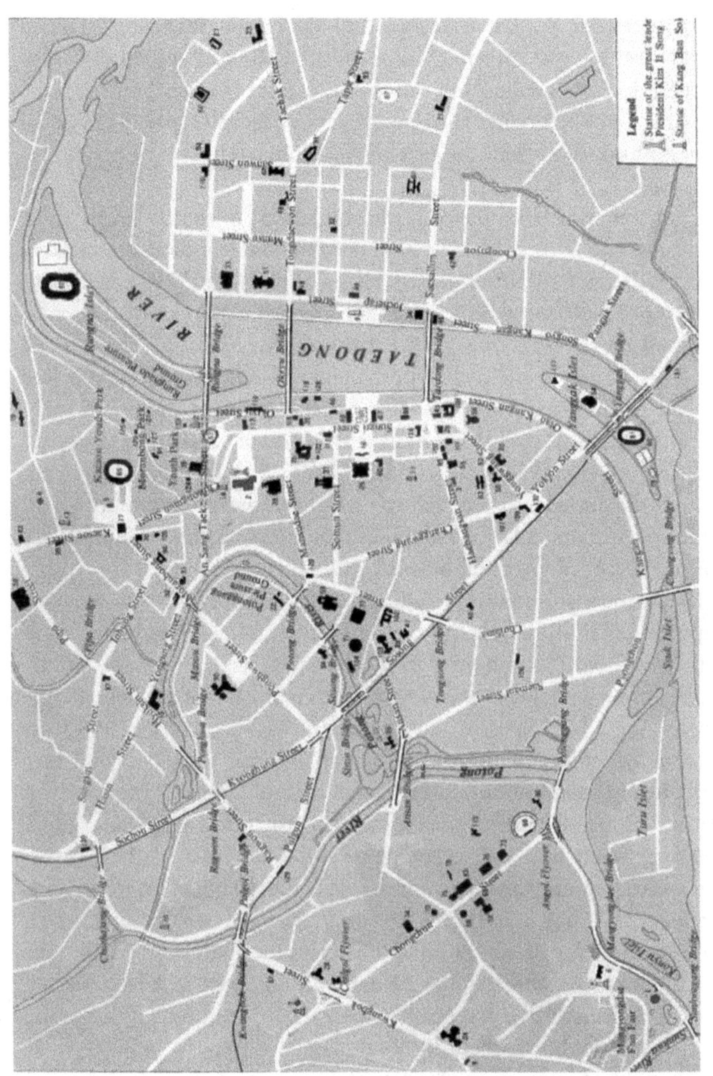

Map of Pyongyang circa 2010.

We arrived at the UNDP office and walked through the UNDP compound which would become our daily environment. There was the two-story office building sited on a slight incline above the entrance road, with a wide circular driveway. The landscaping was nicely designed though nothing was growing under the cold November sky. The office building looked serious but not intimidating, unlike some of the imposing architecture in Pyongyang. Across the road stood the Swedish Embassy and to our left, the Friendship club, comprising a restaurant and a bar.

Upon entering the office, I was immediately struck by its poor condition. The walls seemed to hold onto the stale air of abandonment, a quiet indictment of the years lost. Most furniture had been taken away, water pipes had frozen and burst, and the paint peeled off the walls. When all the international staff left the country in 1997, the Service Bureau, the agency responsible for managing foreign organizations, had stopped maintaining the premises – perhaps out of disappointment over our departure, perhaps as a silent assertion of control or just maybe because the General Services Bureau didn't have the resources. Walking through the gutted rooms, I felt the weight of bureaucracy and recent history pressing in, a useful reminder that our work here would always be at the mercy of forces far beyond our control.

The second substantial building on the compound was a nicely proportioned if unimaginative two-story dwelling. Our apartment was on the first floor (second floor in the United States), a pleasant, roomy one-bedroom apartment full of light from many windows, with a large terrace. The water pipes in our apartment had been spared the frost because the office on the ground floor, hosting the UN Food and Agriculture Organization (FAO) had remained open. However, even with water, our apartment was somewhat worn down. It was a good, solid apartment in a well-constructed building. Parts of the parquet floor were gone, and anything removable had been taken, from curtains to cutlery. We had months of camping ahead, living without much comfort, while repairs to both the office and the apartment would take time to complete. Outside, the garden had not been tended to either. Carolyn noticed a large greenhouse in disrepair and decided that come spring, we should do something about it.

I thought of contacting Headquarters to report this situation. But then I remembered: North Korea was very, very far away – not just in miles. HQ tended to keep as much distance as possible from any potential mess. They sent staff into programme countries to handle it.

Meanwhile Carolyn showed no such qualms. After eight home installations, this one was by no means the simplest but at least it would be *sans* children. We started negotiating with the Service Bureau for urgent repairs to the office and the house. The negotiations with the Service Bureau were complex in that we had not expected so many repairs for our home (the same applied to the office: HQs did not expect the state of disrepair of the office building, nor the bills we asked them to pay for their share of the renovation, notably for equipment that could not be procured locally). An essential component of these negotiations centred on what the GSB would pay and what currency would be used: local North Korean *won* (NKW) or convertible euros or yen (US dollars were not much in use during my stay in North Korea). We would reimburse the GSB with euros for equipment purchased abroad and with local *won* for labour and local materials. The GSB would suggest outrageous rates of exchange which amounted dangerously close to paying in foreign currency. As individuals however, we were doing our best to find better rates when purchasing Korean Won.

My operations colleagues in the office would do marvel in procuring and importing equipment themselves, mostly in China. At home, we eventually upgraded the kitchen courtesy IKEA Beijing, and we improved the bathroom by buying a large rubber trash can to keep full of clean water at all times, to ease the uncertainty of the plumbing situation. Carolyn could hang her signature large print on the living room wall, a stylized, colorful and (to Americans) still recognizable Jasper Johns painting of an abstract map of the USA.

Just as we began to plan for furniture and equipment shopping, the second unpleasant surprise hit. We had understood that we could procure furniture locally. But, without warning, a sudden reform of the local currency – the won – caught us completely off guard. During the night of 30 November 2009, the NKW100 you held became just NKW1. Worse still, foreign currencies like the euro or Japanese yen were no longer allowed. The Government had undertaken this drastic measure to control inflation and eliminate foreign currencies from the economy. Experts speculated that Kim Jong Il was unhappy with an emerging middle class, holding foreign currencies and tasting economic freedom. The redenomination was a brutal reminder of who held power. Or, as some wrote, was it an effort to curb corruption, or to prepare for 2012: the Year of Juche 101?[1]

The country seemed to descend into a North Korean version of chaos – though 'chaos' here was not what one might expect elsewhere.

There were no riots or open protests – just quieting, urgent desperation. We watched Pyongyang's residents move with feverish determination, rushing to any open store to buy whatever they could – oil, furniture... anything that might hold value. One particular scene stuck with me: a woman standing in front of a padlocked store, her face a mask of frustration and anger. Her silence, and the resigned expressions of those around her, made it all the more unsettling. I couldn't help but wonder how many of them had endured this kind of upheaval before – how many had learned the hard way that the ground beneath their feet could shift in an instant? Prices did fluctuate wildly, from NKW138 to NKW40 to the euro within a week, and in one case, even within a single day at a hotel in Pyongyang. Rumours swirled that people had been throwing *won* into the river, desperate to rid themselves of currency that had lost its value.

After a few days, buying anything, including food, proved more difficult.[2] Oddly enough, one of the three restaurants in Munsudong did manage to open its doors from time to time. Someone said that its manager had close ties to a high-ranking Party official. That restaurant served homestyle Asian cooking such as stir-fried vegetable or tofu over rice. The western food was more touch and go. It was however for the North Koreans that things became even more difficult, including the people we interacted with. One new local staff asked me to buy them bread. Such a request never happened afterwards. One older officer in the MFA didn't even try to hide his anxiety when discussing the food situation with me.

In the end, the government adjusted its policy. In December, salaries were distributed at the same rate as before the redenomination, as if the two zeros had never been cut. Salaries were estimated to be between NKW5,000 and NKW10,000 per month – roughly equivalent to USD1–3 based on the black-market exchange rates at the time. The Government also issued a subsidy of NKW800 to the entire population, which was enough to buy 200 grammes of rice. Additionally, they raised the ceiling on how much new currency could be exchanged.[3] The Government had realized they couldn't undo changes that had already taken root: people had come to rely on markets, called *jangmadang*, where individuals could sell food items. These markets could range from ad hoc roadside stalls to organized markets like the Tong-il market, which foreigners could visit.

Despite this reversal, the damage was done. In the months that followed this failed reform, we continued to witness hunger, inflation, and the ongoing marketization of society. Kim Jong Il had failed to completely regain his grip on the economy. Someone had to be held responsible for the debacle and it had to be at level of the Workers' Party of Korea (WPK), also known as the Korean Workers' Party, the ruling political party of North Korea and the dominant force in the country, controlling the Government, military, and much of North Korean society. According to reports, Pak Nam Gi, the Director of Finance for the Korean Workers Party, was made a scapegoat for the policy failure and was never seen again. But Kim Jong Il's message was clear: survival required caution, and attempts to enrich oneself were risky.

Aside from the stress this episode added to our installation, the currency redenomination was a clarifying moment: people were always one ideological whim away from seeing any personal gain wiped away. The second lesson, however, was that even the North Korean regime had to pay some heed to its population.

* * *

Another early lesson was the need to be ever-watchful with our communications and avoid trying to please the Government in order to score easy points. Mr Song met me in the lobby of the stately Pothonggang hotel as I was about to drive to the office. We talked in front of an enormous painting of Kim Il-Sung and Kim Jong Il standing in front of a beautiful mountain. Song handed me a piece of paper. It was a list of UNDP projects.

'These projects were suspended in 2007. They must resume immediately,' Song started, pressing a list into my hand. It was as if he expected this to be done by tomorrow morning. I looked at the list. It included projects scheduled to resume, yes, but also projects that had been deliberately omitted. The reason for their exclusion was their heavy technological components, such as a Geographic Information System using satellite technology. In the new context of the re-opening, any project with a potential for technology transfer was considered frozen. Mr Song's request caught me. He did not make a distinction between projects even though the Executive Board had specifically listed those that could be resumed. Either he hadn't been briefed, or there was another reason. He was certainly trying to see if more projects could resume, but my instinct told me that he was also testing me and that my ability to function in this country for the next few years depended upon how I would respond.

I took a deep breath. I had never been particularly confrontational. A born compromiser and mediator, I was 'brought up' by UN senior officers who had accompanied the great wave of decolonization of the

1960s and who held very high the host country's right to independence. My first manager in UNDP Vietnam, who had seemed to me very old at the time and who worked for the UN when the Belgian Congo gained independence, instilled in me that the UN would respect countries' sovereignty at all costs. From my first posting in Vietnam, I had experienced the UN as the first and perhaps best partner to bring in Western aid to this isolated, war-torn country. This was my frame of mind when Mr Song bluntly placed the list of projects in my hand. I knew however that I had better speak now, or risk weeks of assumptions calcifying into policy that would never be implemented.

'Mr. Song, as you know, the office is reopening with a new setup. We can restart some, but not all, projects.' Song listened without reaction. I gave no details on which projects or timelines. I expected that my response would cause enough issues with the Government.

In the meantime, I had to stop focusing on UNDP exclusively. New requests had intervened and required that I start paying attention to my responsibilities on behalf of other UN Agencies.[Map of Pyongyang]

Chapter 3

A Failed Peace Mission

Personnel challenges – A first look at the humanitarian situation – Pascoe visit – UN flag

The Six Party Talks involved North Korea, the United States, China, Russia, South Korea and Japan. They began after North Korea quit the Nuclear Non-Proliferation Treaty in 2003. China played a crucial role in the Six-Party Talks, serving as both a host and a key mediator, aiming to achieve denuclearization of the Korean peninsula and to maintain peace and stability in the region. While the talks ultimately stalled, China's involvement was vital in bringing North Korea to the negotiating table and facilitating dialogue. Between 2003 and 2007, five rounds of talks pushed Pyongyang to shut down its nuclear facilities in exchange for fuel aid and steps toward normalization with the US and Japan. But in April 2009, the UN Security Council condemned the North Korean failed satellite launch, prompting the DPRK to pull out of Six Party Talks, resume its nuclear enrichment programme and expel all nuclear inspectors from the country.

* * *

As soon as I could, I met the UN agencies working on North Korea. My first goal was to introduce myself and discuss the humanitarian situation. The UN agencies form a Country Team (UNCT) which coordinates its programme on the ground and addresses any emergencies. The UNCT prepares a multiyear plan, allocates funding, oversees thematic groups (which include the Government and other organizations) on Agriculture, Health, Water and other sectors.

I soon found out that the job of UN Coordinator was a strange hybrid. On the one hand, as Representative, I headed one Agency, UNDP, and on the other as Coordinator, I was expected to harmonize the work of existing UN agencies that did not report to me. Since its inception in 1945, the UN system has expanded organically, often resulting in overlapping mandates at the country level. The UN

Coordinator, empowered by the Secretary-General, aims to align various agencies towards a unified goal despite their individual budgets and personnel controls, by organizing thematic working groups and drafting joint plans. In non-emergency countries, coordination is primarily managed by the host Government, such as I observed with India's decisive approach to field agencies. In humanitarian emergencies or if host nations have reduced governmental capacity, however, the UN's role in coordination becomes more critical. In such cases, the UN is expected to take the primary role in managing centralized humanitarian resources efficiently. This was the case during my assignments to Cambodia at the height of UN and NGOs presence in the 1990s, and Yemen during the civil war started in the mid 2010s. North Korea fell into the latter category because so much of the UN programming depended upon centralized humanitarian funding and so little came from the organizations' own funds.

During our first UNCT meeting, Mads, the departing WFP Representative and *de facto* coordinator, must have sensed my hesitancy borne from a lack of experience. While he was more senior and experienced than me, he took on a positive and encouraging tone as he walked me through the team dynamics. I quickly realized that to succeed I needed to add value to the work of each Agency, ensuring that the distribution of funds was fair and well-organized, and help each agency to address whatever problems and restrictions were imposed upon them by the government.

The famine of the 1990s marks the time when the world's humanitarian NGOs and international organizations first entered the DPRK. The whole of the DPRK's population bears the memory of this terrible event, which had happened only fifteen years earlier. I noticed throughout my stay its lasting impact on my Korean colleagues. I felt at times that there were limits to what the Government could inflict on its people, and one such limit was to never return to the state of the 1990s.[1]

The North Korean famine, known as the 'Arduous March', lasted from 1994 to 1998. It combined mass starvation with total economic collapse, fuelled by mismanagement, the loss of Soviet support, and repeated natural disasters. Out of 22 million people, somewhere between 250,000 and 3 million died – with deaths peaking in 1997. As soon as 1991, after severe food shortages led to a lowering of the Public Distribution System (PDS) ration, Pyongyang called in the WFP to conduct a needs assessment. However, on the ground, the WFP met with a lack of cooperation. In 1991 it was still impossible for the political elite to admit to a failure in Government economic policy. Rations continued to be

Table 3.1 The UN System during my tenure in the DPRK

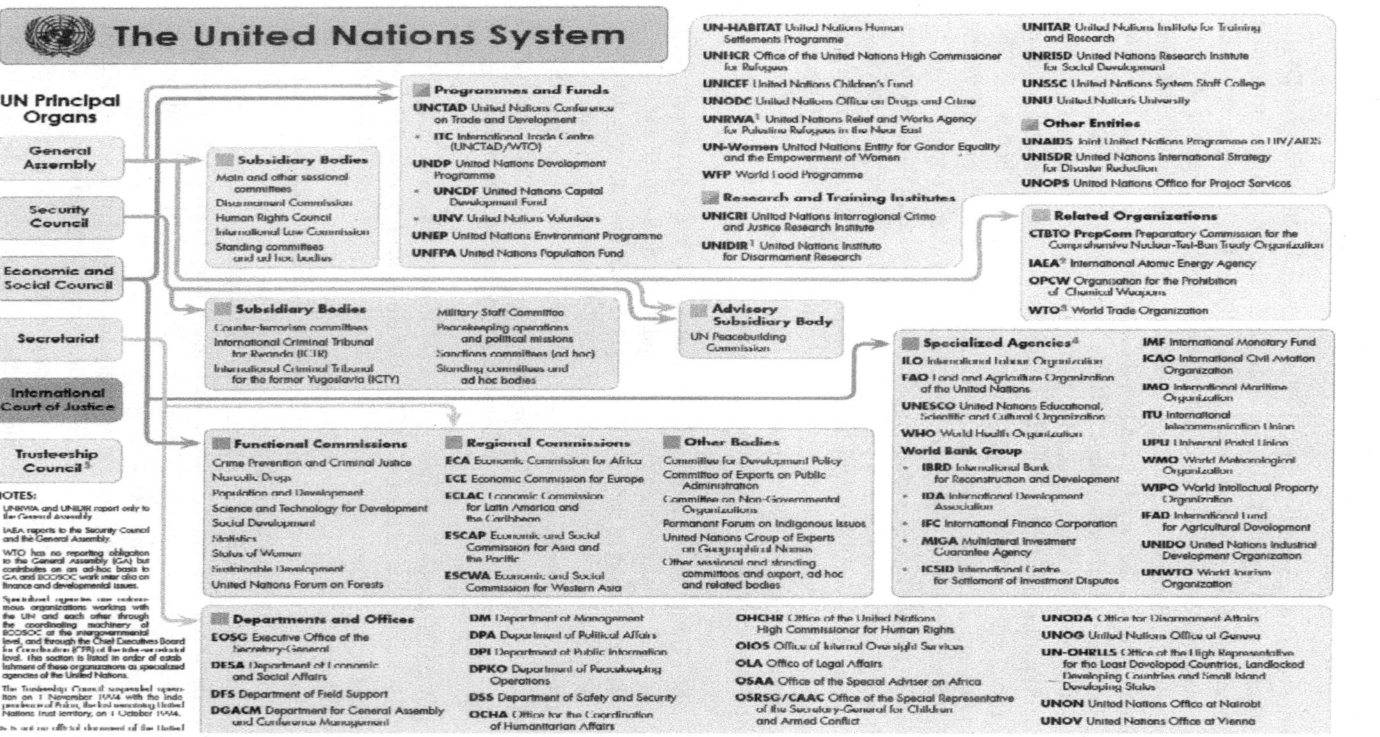

Note: Because the UN System has so many programmes and activities, it can appear quite cumbersome to the host country and local UN team.

reduced throughout the early 1990s. Eventually, in 1995, the DPRK authorities did appeal to foreign assistance. The catastrophe prompted the arrival of the UN and international NGOs. Beginning in 1996, the US also started shipping food aid to North Korea through the WFP to combat the famine. Shipments peaked in 1999 at nearly 600,000 tons making the US the largest foreign aid donor to the country at the time.

Mads started the discussion. 'Half of North Korean households have lived in constant food insecurity,' he explained. 'In many parts of the country, almost half of the children show the miserable, tell-tale signs of chronic malnutrition: stunted growth, thin hair, soft bones . . .' The population most at risk was those fully dependent on the Public Distribution System (PDS), or 16 million out of a total population of 24 million people. Life expectancy had fallen to 66 years, a full 14 years less than in South Korea and 10 years less than China. These were shocking statistics for Northeast Asia when compared to the game-changing progress of China or South Korea, especially during the past 30 years.

He continued with his explanation for the situation, focusing on the chronic nature of vulnerabilities in the DPRK:

> The country just cannot feed its population by itself: 80 per cent of the land is mountains, there is no equipment or fertilizer and all it takes for hunger to spread is for a slight change in weather to delays crops. I am not even talking about natural disasters such as droughts, floods, tidal surges, hailstorms, or typhoons, that are frequent in this part of the world. North Korean agriculture is unprotected: no safety net, no strategic reserves or financial aid, no emergency imports.

I thought I could have completed his answer: '*The well-being of the people would require obtaining food and equipment from abroad, which means being on good terms, or at least trading with the rest of the world.*'

Edward, our FAO colleague, spoke next. He was an experienced agronomist from the UK. He was also a dedicated bird-watcher who took us on early morning walks through the parks of Pyongyang in search of cuckoos, swifts or fowls. Edward explained that this past year, North Korea had entered the 'lean season' late, a period of time when reserves from the previous Autumn crop were depleted and people went hungry. He said that the North Korean climate reminded him of northern Europe when cold temperatures during the Spring season could go into May or even June. If the weather was too cold, the North Korean farmers risked waiting too long to organize the germination of seedlings (rice and maize) and to prepare agricultural fields, spread

Figure 3.1 Working in the rice fields in May, South Hamgyong Province. Photo by Jerome Sauvage.

fertilizer/organic compost and transplant seedlings. In such case, the Spring crop was late, creating food shortages. It had happened this year.

Although the Spring crop represented only five per cent of the average annual cereal output, it was essential to cover the hunger gap between the end of food reserves (used up during winter) and October, when finally the main harvest was available. Although we didn't as yet have the full numbers on the main harvest, Edward repeated that in his estimation, people had surely experienced hunger this year. The logic was clear, but my thoughts drifted beyond the numbers. What did that delay mean on the ground? Were families already stretching rations, skipping meals?

During these tough, lean months, Edward explained, the population depended a lot more upon critical survival strategies. Some people coped by asking for food from their relatives from cooperative farms, others foraged wild food from the fields and mountains, and those living by the sea would collect seaweed. Following the severe food shortages of the mid- and late-1990s and the inability of the Public Distribution System to deliver full food rations, North Koreans also started to grow food in kitchen gardens and on uncultivated slopes of mountains for their own consumption. Each household on the cooperative farm was allowed to tend to a private kitchen garden of about 100 m^2, sometimes through their work units. In cities, a significant proportion of people also had access to smaller garden plots. A typical pattern of cultivation in these gardens constituted of an early crop of potatoes and green corn, followed by vegetables such as cabbage, peppers, radish and garlic. Also following the famine of the 1990s, some of the most vulnerable groups, like the elderly, were informally allowed to cultivate sloping land in excess of 15 degrees.

We continued the briefing with the UNICEF Representative, Arjun, a dynamic and experienced professional from South Asia. Arjun and I shared the fact that we were both first-time Representatives and that our daughters had been in school in New Delhi together. Although UNICEF took the lead in several areas in health, notably combating TB and malaria, his presentation centred on his agency's projects in water and sanitation, in collaboration with four other NGOs from France, the UK, Ireland, and Germany.[2] Spring was the peak season for water and sanitation project activities in the field, just as winter eased and before the busy harvest time. Rural sanitation was, of course, a key concern for sanitation experts. In North Korea the almost complete lack of fertilizer forced farmers to use night-soil, a polite euphemism for human excrement used to fertilize vegetable gardens. That was a risky practice, causing disease. Arjun explained that because the poorest North Koreans were chronically undernourished, they were more susceptible to illness and increased mortality rates.

The result of this malnutrition and poor water sanitation, was that, on a societal level, the North Korean population suffered from stunted growth and even decreased cognitive development. Arjun paused, looked at everyone, then: 'This means that as exposure to food deprivation goes on under these conditions, North Koreans experience what scientists call 'transgenerational epigenetic inheritance of hunger'. In layman terms, each generation sees its development stunted because its ability to fight the risk of diseases and overall longevity is affected'.[3] We became silent, trying to digest the idea of malnutrition modifying the genetic make-up of a nation.

I turned to Dr. Alina, a dedicated doctor from central Asia, trained in Russia who worked as WHO's Health Emergency Coordinator. In my years in Pyongyang, I would learn a lot from Alina. In her home country, she was a leading University professor who trained young doctors in Maternal and Child Health. In Pyongyang, she would occasionally provide backup medical doctor to expatriate women who needed care.

'I am afraid I cannot give you better news about North Korea's healthcare system,' she said.

> On the one hand, we have in North Korea a cadre of committed personnel, excellent understanding of basic hygiene and care and even many diseases that are preventable, such as TB and hepatitis B. But the health system has been in crisis since the mid-1990s. Chronic shortages of medicine, equipment, and trained professionals. You will see for yourself how hospitals often lack even the most basic supplies, such as antibiotics, anaesthesia, and sterilized surgical tools, forcing doctors to perform procedures without proper sanitation or pain relief. Power outages are so frequent that surgeries are sometimes conducted by candlelight, and X-ray machines sit idle due to lack of electricity.[4]

'Outside of Pyongyang,' Alina continued,

> conditions are even worse. Rural clinics often consist of a single doctor with no medicine to offer beyond herbal remedies or outdated pills. To receive basic treatment, patients need to pay in cash, or with cigarettes. The state-run pharmaceutical industry produces only a fraction of the necessary medicines, leaving desperate citizens to rely on the black market, where counterfeit drugs are common.

As we were leaving, Mads paused and said to me, 'The challenge – and the tragedy – of our mission is double: on the one hand, millions of people depend upon a State that doesn't place their survival as its first priority. On the other hand, all the aid from NGOs, bilateral and international organizations represents a much lower amount than in any other country around the world that experience similar deprivation.'

* * *

Aside from the physical rehabilitation of the office, one of my priorities was to build the UNDP team from scratch, which meant bringing in a few more international staff and recruiting the team of North Korean personnel. The UNDP Board had approved the office's reopening, but only on the condition that certain measures would be taken to avoid repeating past mistakes. One of those conditions involved selecting and contracting North Korean personnel. I was tasked with negotiating the implementation of these conditions with the MFA. I requested a meeting with Mr Yun Tae Song, the head of the international department, whom I had yet to meet. From what I'd heard, he was a well-placed figure within the Korean Workers Party, close to the centre of power, and quite powerful in his own right.

The drive to the MFA took about ten minutes from Munsudong. We arrived at an immense square bordered by massive Soviet-style buildings, each the length of a city block. There were no commercial stores, only these enormous structures and a palace facing the river and, beyond the river, the imposing Juche Tower. The palace had a curved roof, reminiscent of traditional Korean palatial architecture. Huge portraits of Marx and Engels adorned the tops of some buildings. Other than for one or two cars and a few bicycles, the gigantic square was empty.

A young man was waiting for us in front of the MFA. He ushered us through a marble hall and into a meeting room, where two men sat at a long table beneath a panoramic painting of Kim Jong Il standing on a rock, gazing out over fierce ocean waves that lay at his feet like tamed dogs. Under the painting sat Mr Yun Tae Song, his grey suit impeccably tailored, a 555 cigarette – favoured in the region – resting between his fingers.

The meeting would address changes that had never been attempted before in the cooperation between the DPRK and international organizations. The first change consisted in hiring, paying and managing local staff ourselves. Up to now, in North Korea, every foreign agency was assigned local personnel who they neither selected nor paid and who came from – and directly reported to – their national ministries. Traditionally foreign organizations did not have the option of selecting local staff required to carry out projects and conduct day-to-day business. They were required to use personnel from the North Korean Government, which it selected and assigned for a period of time. Staff came either from the DPRK's MFA or from a technical Ministry and they retained their affiliation with the ministries that employed them.

The North Korean side expressed some concern with the setup that we proposed, but we found solutions to each of their objections. When they argued that their economy did not include private employment and therefore private contracts, we submitted our own contract models and adjusted the language. We found a solution to the absence of a true labour pool: we prepared job descriptions and advertised openings throughout the Government and among other aid organizations. When we asked candidates to complete the standard UN 'Personal History Form', I began to realize how odd some of these processes might have appeared to them. For example, we asked whether they would experience any limitation to travelling abroad (question 10 on the form), if they had taken steps to change residence in another country than their own, or to change their nationality (questions 16 and 17); or if they had been arrested or summoned into court (question 32)! We duly conducted interviews and hired North Korean staff with official letters of contract entailing terms of employment, salary, etc. We ran a local salary survey to establish a pay structure. How were we going to pay our new personnel in a country without a banking system? It took us weeks of creative negotiations to open accounts in the Foreign Trade Bank. It felt like we were opening a private account inside the Bank of England, or the US Federal Reserve.

Out of the recruitment process came a dynamic young woman to work with me. She was motivated and active behind the scene, to ease things out for the whole office. She was curious about projects and soon became our focal point on gender issues, driving a hard bargain with seasoned male programme officers to make sure that they paid more attention to the place of women in their projects. She was supportive of Carolyn's activities.

The special administrative status given the UNDP local staff apparently gave them some prestige among their cohort also working at other NGOs and agencies. I did experience limits to my authority, however, when I met the head of the international department Mr Yun Tae Song, and was accompanied by Kim Ri Sol, my most senior local staff member. There, I soon realized that I would have to compete for my direct supervisee's attention with his 'other supervisor', that is to say, Mr Yun! This realization of the limits of a UN affiliation was reinforced every morning when we observed the staff arrive at the office in a minivan, alight from the van and show their papers to the guards at the office area's entrance before entering. Carolyn and I found this process deeply humiliating for the staff.

UN contracts or not, the situation made for strange work relationships and raised the question as to whether our Korean colleagues followed our Agency's rules or those of the North Korean Government. Over time, I observed how adeptly they managed these contradictions. They appeared to have developed a sort of double personality under which each 'persona' truly believed in its respective mission. It sometimes led to a kind of double-think/double-speak. When that worked well, our national colleagues displayed an impressive ability to synthetize the Government's and our side of an issue into a coherent, workable whole. At other times however, they appeared to have more difficulty speaking simply about what to me seemed like an uncontroversial issue. When that happened, they'd revert to some automatic, default-like, slogan-sounding response. I remember an example when we were developing our programme. I suggested that UNDP offices around the world frequently organized events that we called 'policy dialogues' and which enabled a Government to discuss economic and social issues with world-class experts. I could not get our Korean colleagues to agree to the idea. They were hemming and hawing. Finally, after I pushed harder for an answer, one of them stiffened and said, 'In our country, policy can only be determined by our Leader. It does not get to be discussed, or evaluated.' There came another lesson in understanding the country. And finally, if I really pushed, during a one-to-one conversation, into really uncomfortable territory, like trying to discuss the political prison camps, or *Kwanliso*, their face would form into a sort of uncomprehending expression, not unlike that of a teenage child in front of questioning parents, and I knew I had lost them.

For my part, I was beginning to understand that UN neutrality and governmental sovereignty, while noble principles, weren't always sufficient. There were instances when I had to choose a side and demand that the North Korean counterpart understand my position, or getting railroaded back into errors of the past.

* * *

My hope that the UN could play a role for peace was frustrated after the UN Under-Secretary-General for Political Affairs, Lynn Pascoe, visited soon after my arrival in Pyongyang. A former US Ambassador with extensive experience in Moscow and Beijing and who spoke Chinese, Pascoe explained that he had full access to US President Obama as well as to the UN Secretary-General. With the latter's blessing, Pascoe was in charge of prevention and resolution of conflicts around the world. With his experience and responsibilities, he could hope to make some progress in the deadlock between the DPRK and the Security Council. We hastily put a programme together. He arrived in Pyongyang with two South Korean advisers in tow, including the right-hand man to UN Secretary-General Ban Ki-moon, Kim Won-soo.

The delegation arrived in Pyongyang and was immediately transported to one of the houses operated by the MFA, in the heart of Pyongyang. Pascoe suggested that I stay with the delegation for the duration of the mission. I did, but despite the elegant classical Korean mansion surrounded by a dense park, it felt like house arrest, especially without access to internet. Pascoe and Kim Won-soo's trip seemed to me like a last attempt to convince the DPRK to come back to the Six Party Talks.

Pascoe wanted me next to him because he hoped to facilitate a deal on behalf of the UN Security Council. The arrangement would include the incentive of a more ambitious agenda of economic development, on the condition that the North Koreans re-entered a dialogue on denuclearization. Hearing this, two contradictory thoughts came to me: on the one hand, yes, I would love to see North Korea's 'Great Opening' with the UN at the forefront of economic reforms projects. After all, North Korea's humanitarian crisis was chronic, structural, and a response would require long-term reforms and development. It would also be necessary to loosen the sanctions that hampered our work on a daily basis.

I was concerned with how tying international financial and development aid to the denuclearization agenda risked making international support more fraught with misunderstandings, more haphazard. When things went well geopolitically, we could make plans, contact donors, offer projects to the North Koreans. But what if something happened – a border incident, a missile test? Would conditionalities inherent in such deals automatically kick in, scuttle our plans and dash our hopes? What of our credibility at the country level if the Security Council dismissed our programmes out of hand?

Pascoe's mission did not start well. Whenever the North Koreans were reluctant to engage into serious conversations, the hapless visitors became likely to experience the 'Pyongyang run-around', as I came to call it: Pascoe and his team toured Pyongyang by car, placed flowers before the statue of Kim Il Sung, appreciated a performance given by the State Symphony Orchestra, visited the Three Tombs of Kangso, the E-Library at Kimchaek University of Technology, the Institute of remote sensing and geo-informatics and the State Academy of Science. At least, they also visited UN-assisted project sites such as a food factory with the WFP and the Pyongyang Maternity Hospital with UNICEF, WHO and UNFPA.

After two days of visits, Ambassador Pascoe and his team became very frustrated with the lack of serious discussion. They asked to meet Leader Kim Jong Il, but this was denied early on. They asked to at least meet two key players in the negotiations with the United States : either Kim Gye Gwan, the first vice foreign minister, who served as chief nuclear envoy in the Six-Party Talks or Kang Sok Ju, who sat alongside Kim Jong Il during his interactions with foreign leaders. At the end of their mission, finally, they were able to meet with Mr Kim Kye Gwan, but the meeting did not seem to produce any tangible result.

At one meeting however, with Vice Foreign Minister Pak Gil Yon, the North Koreans bluntly expressed their views. Vice Minister Pak first quickly disposed of the 'sugar candy' offer of development aid. The North Koreans, he said, separated in their analysis the Security Council from humanitarian and development organizations. To them, these field agencies were global, country-based source of expertise operating under the UN General Assembly. Indeed, the Governing Boards of UN Agencies and Funds are funded by the totality of the members of the General Assembly. On the other end of the spectrum was the Security Council. He described how the Security Council was controlled by the United States and unfriendly towards the DPRK. He was probably still smarting from the fact that China had supported SC decisions against the DPRK three years earlier that had imposed sanctions and an arms embargo.

As to the United States, although Pascoe wanted Pak to believe that the Obama Administration would be open to the Six-Party Talks resuming, he was not able to provide any guarantee from the US President. Obama was just starting his first term, facing a merciless Republican opposition and was not going to spend his fledgling credibility on an elusive and risky peace process with the DPRK. Two years later, starting his second term, Obama accepted the Leap Day agreement with which the UN agencies (WFP) were involved. By then, too much had happened, the DPRK had moved on and the agreement never materialized.

Vice Foreign Minister Pak then directly referred to UN Secretary General Ban Ki-moon. He acknowledged his pride at seeing a Korean become Secretary General of the UN. But, he said, disillusionment followed. 'With each Security Council meeting, we observe the Secretary-General's behaviour. All he has to do when the Council discusses North Korea is to step out of the room. Not for long, but just long enough. He knows it. Yet he's never done it. To us, it does not show an interest in true cooperation at the political level.'

Shortly after Ambassador Pascoe's departure, on the 21st of the same month, North Korea vowed not to dismantle its nuclear programme – not even in exchange for economic aid – as long as the United States continued a 'hostile policy'.[5]

I could understand Pak's frustration with Ban Ki-moon's inability to play a more proactive role for the Korean peninsula. The DPRK assumed that Ban Ki-moon was in a unique position to advance the peace agenda. If this was a last-chance attempt at resuming the Six Party Talks, shouldn't he have done more than sending his lieutenants on what seemed like a perfunctory mission? It is possible that Ban Ki-moon's decision to hold back was related to his potential candidacy for the 2017 South Korean presidential election; in the end, he decided not to run just before the elections. As a Korean, he had a unique card to play, and did not.

On a more positive side, this experience showed me that the UN could play a key role for peace in isolated places where, as in the DPRK, superpowers like the United States or China were not disposed or not able to make such diplomacy happen. The UN has at its disposal a range of tools and measures – from the UN Security Council to organizations working at the country level – that could have real impact. But for that to happen, member countries had to be ready to support them, and the leadership inside the UN had to throw everything in, including their own career considerations.

* * *

It had been a bit of a rough start. The team – both internationals and Korean – was not completely in place. Our living and working premises were still rudimentary. And the Deputy Secretary General's peace mission to the DPRK had not been a success. I needed some encouragement and found it by chance. In the apartment, I discovered a small, yet essential, piece of history: the old UN flag, unceremoniously stuffed in a drawer in my apartment. I smoothed it out and proudly had it hung on the mast in front of the office, under the grey skies of Pyongyang.

Chapter 4

THE SINKING

Sinking of *Cheonan* corvette – Introducing Leni – Trying to understand North Korea's decision-making – Impact on UN Agencies – A word on UN sanctions

Although North and South Korea agreed to a cease fire in 1953, they never signed a peace treaty, leaving all their issues unsettled. Legally, North and South Korea are still at war. A Demarcation Line, the DMZ, separates them, not a border. In the Western Sea, as the DPRK names the more generally-referred Yellow Sea, that line is called The Northern Limit Line, or NLL. The NLL was not agreed upon during the armistice talks and remains disputed today. The coastline and islands on both sides of the NLL are heavily militarized. In such unresolved situations, soon enough bad stuff happens.

* * *

On a cold morning in March, as with most news regarding North Korea, I first learned about the naval incident while listening online during breakfast. A 1,200-tonne South Korean corvette, the *Cheonan*, had been sunk near the NLL, in the aftermath of what was assumed to be a confrontation with the North. 46 South Korean sailors died. Here in Pyongyang, the distance between the quiet reality we faced and the turmoil unfolding on international news channels felt strange. The country I was living in had engaged militarily with its neighbour and yet, around me, all was quiet. Should we be afraid? Should we alert someone? I remember wondering whether I was being complacent, too easily adapting, or if there simply wasn't much we could do. In fact, at the office, the local staff did not know about it for a few more hours. The propaganda machine was always careful to prepare such announcements carefully. I tried to assess the risks to the international community. Could this escalate into a conflict? Another critical responsibility I shouldered concerned staff security. Quietly, I reviewed our security plan and the provisions for evacuation, but South Korea did not escalate. They wanted to establish what exactly had happened before laying blame on the North. This was a relief.

The consequences of the incident began to take clearer shape, particularly within the context of humanitarian work. The UNCT met to discuss security measures and the impact of the *Cheonan* sinking on our operations. It didn't not take long for me to find that the sinking was going to cause problems for our work on the ground and, in turn for the most vulnerable people who expected our aid. The new WFP Country Director, Leni, had just arrived in country and joined us. She was a tall German woman, of proud bearing with kind, green eyes matching her classy silver hair kept in a bun. Her quiet demeanour and even temperament put me at ease. We instantly recognized a kinship in each other: same generation and European upbringing. She knew French and I, some German. We became friends and learned to respect each other throughout our years in the DPRK and beyond. I formally welcomed Leni into our small team, then we started our assessment of the situation. Leni's arrival marked a moment of reflection, not only about the immediate crisis but also on the deeper questions about North Korea's leadership and its broader implications.

'Let's first discuss the incident,' I started. 'I can't help wondering why Leader Kim Jong Il would choose this time of modestly flourishing inter-Korean cooperation to send dozens of South Korean sailors to their death and make life even harder for his people?'

FAO office director Edward, a long-term student of the DPRK, offered a possible explanation.

'Of course,' he began, 'I have not 'read' over what the senior command of the Korean People's Army (KPA) thought.[1] Perhaps they do not want a reconciliation with the South. Perhaps they're not versed in what is happening in the rest of the world, or do not care.' He mentioned the thesis of competing groups vying for power inside the regime. Indeed, analysts have since described the KPA as a semi-autonomous group with opportunity and cause to provoke this incident, independently from the Leader.[2]

His suppositions did not relieve my concern with how our projects might get impacted. As the conversation continued, I couldn't shake a feeling that our work was facing headwinds.

'How does the regime coordinate its international priorities?' I asked. 'It would have seemed to me that it valued their collaborative economic development with South Korea! Now, this cooperation will come undone.'

The Kaesong Industrial Zone was the largest economic link created during 'Sunshine', the period of relaxation of inter-Korean tensions when, between 1998 and 2003, Kim Dae-jung, the first president in South Korea's history to be elected from the opposition, reached out to the North. His 'Sunshine Policy' raised expectations to high levels, fostering family reunions between the two countries and a dialogue between the two Koreas over a peaceful reunification process and culminated in the North–South summit in June 2000 in Pyongyang. The Kaesong Industrial Region was established to allow South Korean businesses to invest in the North. From an economic recovery standpoint the Sunshine Policy also offered hope for grants that would support the DPRK's standard 'social infrastructure'[3]. In the end, the Sunshine Policy failed to deliver on high expectations, as a new generation concerned with economics arose in South Korea and President George W. Bush's opposition marked the end of the Sunshine Policy, followed by the resumption of missiles launches and North Korea's first nuclear test in 2006. For the South, Kaesong was a drop in the bucket economically, but a last remaining vestige towards the goal of reunification[4]. For the North, it was a source of jobs and hard currency, pumping $50 million per month into the North Korean economy. It was also one of the few economic successes that the Government had to show its people.

Christina, our population statistician with the UN Population Agency, intervened. She was a very qualified demographer hailing from Southeast Asia, who had conducted population censuses worldwide and has extensively published. 'Senior military officers attended our meeting on the Census a few weeks ago,' she pointed out. 'They listened intently to our presentations. We mentioned that South Korea financed the Census' and they sounded interested.' She looked worried. 'Is that project dead now?'

Listening to my colleagues, I began to quietly question the humanitarian principles guiding our work in such unstable setting. Neutrality requires aid to be delivered regardless of conflicts, but I now questioned this principle north of the DMZ. The reality in the DPRK was that everything depended upon geopolitical context: the history that brought us there; the funding that supported us; our ability to enter the country and to work inside it. We were here because of geopolitical considerations. And we risked leaving because of those, too.

As the situation developed, indeed, it became more abundantly clear that the sinking would have far-reaching consequences not just for diplomatic relations, but also for funding our ongoing programmes. The South Korean Unification Ministry, in charge of cross-border relations, temporarily suspended spending on projects across 10 Ministries. Some UN agencies' headquarters quietly advised their programme directors and representatives to temporarily ease up on fund-raising messages. Cutbacks on funding would have major implications for us.

For example, UNICEF had planned US$6.3 million worth of projects to improve water and sanitation, but had received so far only US$1.9 million. Australia, one of their most reliable donors, had not provided any funding in the past year and now was not the time to remind them about their promises for the DPRK. In addition, Australia was making their conditions more stringent. They said that they would no longer finance a water sanitation project because it included drilling wells for water. In their view, projects with wells qualified as development work, not emergency aid.

'*But unsafe water kills*,' I said. Arjun nodded, citing research on the topic.[5]

I became increasingly frustrated.

'Any town or city in Australia, Europe or the United States spends millions to prevent raw sewage from coming in contact with citizens' water. Is it too much to ask for $6 million dollars to improve water for a population of 24 million people?'

Arjun nodded sympathetically, 'Donors don't know enough about the difficulties of ordinary North Koreans.' I thought to myself that we might not have done a good enough job letting them know and resolved to work on our communications. I turned to Leni.

'What about WFP?'

'We've received US$2.84 million from the Governments of Switzerland and Brazil, for dried skimmed milk for children.'

Leni continued, 'Other than these funds, we've received only a third of our funding requests for the year. This new situation means that we will probably close a few of WFP's food factories in-country. We will be forced to decide which age groups will not receive food aid: young children, mothers or seniors?'

'How will you decide,' I asked?

'We prioritize based on need,' she answered wearily but firmly. Need was everywhere and prioritization was just another word for choosing who went hungry first. Another agency leader mentioned that unless they could get adequate funding, they might suspend operations altogether.

The Director of WHO spoke next, factually and quietly, but with worry. 'This military incident will remind the world of North Korea's nuclear capabilities. The international response will make importing advanced medical equipment even more difficult than before,' he said. UN Security Council Resolution No. 1718, passed in 2006 and tightened in 2009 after a second test, restricted technical training, services, and manufacturing support. Procurement of essential medical equipment – X-ray machines, TB diagnostic tools, and anaesthesia machines – would stretch from weeks to months. I tried not to think about surgical procedures without anaesthesia. The doctor continued, explaining that every item was vetted against the Prohibited List for dual-use technology.

Dual-use! That phrase soon became a refrain to many of our programme negotiations. Dual-use items refer to any good, software or technology that can be used for both civilian and military applications. Every piece of equipment containing as little as ten per cent of US technology was to be approved by the US Government. Additionally, the UN ban on exports of metals, machinery, and vehicles to North Korea covered several categories of goods common to aid programmes, including agricultural equipment and certain medical supplies.

Of all the agencies, UNDP was especially scrutinized because of its development orientation and of its recent problems with the US Government. We were to abide with the entire sanctions regime, irrespective of the humanitarian exemptions which the UN could claim on a case-by-case basis. And even if an export license was approved, potential suppliers hesitated to bid, wary of having the words 'North Korea' on their financial records. These suppliers did not want to be labelled as a money laundering concern and consequently seeing their assets frozen by the US Government. Global financial institutions closed their North Korean accounts for fear of suffering a similar penalty.

The UN Resolution allowed exemptions on a case-by-case basis for the export of humanitarian goods to North Korea. My colleagues in charge of procurement ended up getting to know very well the people at the US Government's Office of Foreign Assets Control (OFAC). We regularly spoke to them, always to inform them of our plans to purchase specific equipment and to explain their purpose.

At times, complying with sanctions led to absurdities. For example, a Congressional aide once seriously proposed to me that metal sieves for sorting seeds could be used in nuclear machinery. I doubted this, assuming North Korea had access to more suitable technology than repurposing agricultural equipment. An agency found that stainless steel tweezers provided in women's health kits provoked dual-use related questions about their potential use as weapons. These were in my estimation ludicrous concerns that wasted precious procurement time. A colleague on my team, frustrated with the lengthy procurement process, once suggested bypassing it entirely by citing the humanitarian exception in the Resolutions. I would understand his frustration but knew that we could not expose ourselves to any criticism from member States. But I was sympathetic. There were days when the extreme conditions of living in Pyongyang would collide with our small-bore self-imposed rules; it was as if we were operating in an irrational, other-world reality that made our efforts to assist the North Korean people a caricature.

As regards UNDP, the impact on our programme re-launch was particularly felt. When UNDP slowed down our programme development, the Government's representative heatedly responded and I was stuck in the middle. I already knew that the projects carried over from the 2007 suspension would not resume immediately, despite the North Korean Government's expectations, because HQs had insisted they be entirely re-formulated. Had Cheonan not occurred, we could have convinced HQs to proceed with preparatory, immediate actions whilst re-designing the projects. These early preparative activities exist under a special procedure and can take place before full project approval, as long as they remain under certain expenditures ceilings. Early achievements would have gained us credibility whilst negotiating tougher requirements for the full projects, such as monitoring access or community participation. I had been hopeful for a positive response from New York but none came.

The North Korean Government started its grievances with a simple letter expressing concerns about the lead-time to resume the projects, and increased pressure from there. Over the following months, an unrelenting barrage of criticism and acrimony ensued. If I needed to discuss an unrelated issue with higher officials at the MFA, no matter the subject, they would bring up instead the status of our projects. There was nothing I could do but repeat the same thing: 'I understand, but that's the situation. We will get these projects going but it will take a little longer than planned.'

I became so affected by the unrelenting pressure that, one day, meeting with Mr Yun Tae Song, I muttered some excuse, got up and left the room. Mr Yun was shocked. In the car taking me back to the office, although feeling somehow safer, I wondered what I had done and what would happen to me. Truth was, I had had it. I needed to communicate to the Government that the situation could not go on. I knew well that on their side, each person and unit within the MFA had to show results that translated in dollar amounts. They too faced tremendous pressure. Their only way to respond was to apply blunt force on me, hoping that I would make the problems disappear and our projects magically appear. I eventually found a way, but it took many difficult months.

* * *

Aside from making our work problematic and slower, I really could not see how sanctions did anything to prevent North Korea's military nuclear development, as evidenced from a decade of missile and nuclear testing. Sanctions severely impacted the lives of ordinary citizens. Fuel shortages didn't affect the military, who kept its own supply sources and its own reserves. It was ordinary civilians who were forced to walk, push buses instead of riding them, or endure power outages. Reduced kerosene and diesel supplies led to deforestation for biomass fuel, exacerbating erosion, floods, and food shortages. Limited diesel also hampered irrigation, harvesting, food storage and processing, transportation, increasing famine risks.[6] Blocked oil shipments ultimately harmed the North Korean people while likely pushing the country closer to other rich energy countries such as Russia. The need to secure alternative sources of foreign currency no doubt must have played a role in the cyber criminality which developed during my mission in the DPRK[7]. These were not the outcomes the United States and the UN Security Council had expected. It was hard to witness this failure of policy[8].

We could buy Swiss watches costing 3,000 Euros at a Pyongyang store we called the Japanese Store, when ordinary North Koreans had trouble buying small Chinese-made equipment to maintain a water pump. Over the years following my departure, sanctions kept getting tougher. International banking became completely impracticable for international organizations and NGOs. Some brought cash in bags, a needlessly risky operation. Waiting for exemptions from the US could so delay project activities as to render them obsolete.

For the humanitarian community, the imposition of sanctions was no theoretical 'high level' geopolitical action. Their effectiveness proved limited in the case of the DPRK. To those of us trying to implement the most basic of aid projects, sanctions severely hampered our ability to provide, at the local level, tangible help to the North Korean people.

* * *

Two months after the *Cheonan* incident, a team of investigators from Sweden, Australia, Britain, and the United States (and South Korea in a separate report) concluded that a North Korean torpedo sank the ship. Other States, groups and individuals disagreed with the official report (including, perhaps not surprisingly, Russia and China but also scientists at the University of Manitoba) and could not confirm whether the North Korean Navy caused the incident.

In any case, harm was done to our efforts to finance and execute programmes in North Korea. The challenge of explaining our work to the outside world had become even more complicated than before. We had to communicate better with our donors and the world, while working in-country to enhance programme monitoring and accountability. These efforts at greater transparency already faced significant resistance from the North Korean side, who was unwilling to allow foreign agencies poke around their business.

Chapter 5

HEART OF DARKNESS

First visit to the field – A drive to Hoechang – Rural energy –A Korean lunch

North Korea experiences a cool continental climate with distinct seasons. Winters are long and cold, similar to Northern Europe and North America, with mean temperatures ranging from about 20°F (-7°C) in the south to -10°F (-23°C) in the northern interior. Summers are warm and humid, with average July temperatures above the upper 60s°F (about 20°C) in most places.

Anyone visiting the DPRK is sure to notice the lack of electric power. Think of those night-time photos of the Korean Peninsula and China taken from space: North Korea is the dark landmass, as black as the seas surrounding it, a dark passage between brightly lit South Korea and China. Even in the capital, Pyongyang, streetlights work infrequently and inside our homes we could not count on a steady electricity supply. North Korea's energy difficulties started in the early 1990's as support from the Soviet Union ended and despite Chinese coal imports. Since then, the country hasn't invested in its generation or distribution infrastructure. It would take investments in the billions to repair it. Whereas Pyongyang – and to a lesser extent provincial cities – keeps some light on, rural areas experience near complete blackout. This is especially true in winter when the cities need to heat themselves and there is less demand for energy to support harvest. In line with UNDP's new mandate of directly supporting the people with programmes that did not require high technology content, our office was determined to launch rural energy projects as quickly as possible.

* * *

I had the opportunity to take my first visit outside of Pyongyang, to Hoechang County in the Province of South Pyongyan (not to confuse with the Province of Pyongyang, that gave its name to the Capital). Central Government and County officials wished to show us a hydro-power installation upon which some of the county's energy depended, and to ascertain how UNDP might improve their electric generation capacity.

Downstairs, Pak waited with our office's white Toyota Landcruiser. I wondered about the status of our four-wheel drive Landcruiser and Audi during the three-year suspension. Did the cars stay in the garage behind the office or were they utilized and if so, by whom? I never asked Mr Pak probably knowing I would not have received an answer. A young North Korean colleague from the office, Yu Kwang, came along. He was a young man with more hair than was usually authorized in society, wide glasses and enthusiasm that made him a great traveling companion.

I looked at the drive ahead with some apprehension. Interactions with Mr Song had been a little tense so far, but I hoped that getting down to business and planning projects would help. I was relieved to see that Choe Song Ho, who I had already met, would join us. He was different from the rest of the Ministry team. He even dressed differently: beige Docker chinos and a tweed jacket. With his metal-rimmed glasses, you'd more likely expect to meet him on a University campus. His face was open and smiling, under a mass of salt and pepper hair, almost boyish, although the crows-feet at the outer corners of his eyes revealed worry and stress. I realized over time that he was by far the most competent among our counterparts. His role must have added stress to his life. I felt intuitively that he was strongly experiencing the contradiction between what needed to be done and what could not be done. He was a dreamer in a world of brutal realism.

This was an opportunity for me to catch a first glimpse of life outside Pyongyang. Our white Landcruiser bearing the UN flag sped along the northern side of the Taedong River, which runs through Pyongyang towards the Western Sea (as the Koreans call the Yellow Sea). Then we turned east, towards more mountainous areas. Twenty minutes later, we were outside the city on a paved road without cars or trucks to slow us down. On the banks of the river, women and men were washing their clothes, and beyond the river, there was a row of tall bright golden trees, their yellow leaves flying off the branches in the late autumn wind, and beyond them, more hills on the horizon. Heavy clouds moved fast against the pale blue sky and we could feel the approach of winter in the cold air.

A second car with North Korean plates, with representatives of the Ministry of Electric Power Industry, joined us to form a small convoy. We turned right and crossed a bridge over the Taedong River. After the bridge, the road narrowed and became compacted dirt. The cars started to climb uphill as fewer houses lined the road. Travelling east, we followed another river, some tributary to the Taedong River. The sky was now grey, the dark clouds hung low on the hill tops where traces of green persisted. The swollen river rushed through massive boulders. The further we journeyed, the thicker the mist, enveloping us in a cold embrace, and the less people we saw.

The view made me feel lonely, removed from the city we left only an hour ago. A work gang of young men and boys watched us pass, leaning on their shovels or against bicycles, each standing before a heap of rocks or a mound of sand, poised to fill potholes. It's clear that their work will not withstand the next rainfall.

Looking up, I spotted a pylon on the edge of a hill with small cable cars meant to transport coal from a mine. The equipment appeared rusty and motionless. The few houses along the road had low cement walls, whitewashed with two windows and two doors on one side, their roofs covered in grey tile with gently raised edges in the traditional Korean style. The grey tiles were softened with vines that stretched to the top of the roof. Beyond the house, there was an outhouse, a shed, but no chimneys on the roof or electric wires reaching into the house.

Figure 5.1 Road maintenance work crew, South Pyongyan Province. Photo by Jerome Sauvage.

Figure 5.2 House on the road to Hoechang. Photo by Jerome Sauvage.

We passed a man walking on the side of the road. I noticed his trousers of grey canvas, too short for his legs, accentuating his bow-legged gait. Strapped to his back was a traditional Korean A-frame backpack made of wood, held in place by ropes around his shoulders. On the 'seat' of the pack rested an empty potato sack and a traditional hand hoe. I later saw similar hoes and backpacks displayed at the Seoul Folk Museum, as relics of the past. But here, this farmer still used the heavy contraption for its original purpose. I tried to engage my fellow passengers.

'That backpack seems weighty, but the man carries it easily,' I remarked.

'Our farmers have found that these packs are more practical and more durable than the modern ones ' Mr Song answered. 'Our farmers are sturdy and carry these bags by their own choice.'

Me, wanting to sound knowledgeable: 'African women carry food on their heads in beautiful woven baskets, and for long distances.'

'This isn't Africa,' replied Mr Song curtly. 'I was posted in Africa, you know. There is nothing in common between our country and Africa. Foreign organizations often make that mistake. If you want to compare our country, use Europe.'

Unable to think of some polite retort, I stayed quiet, when in the front seat, Mr Choe half turned towards me and issued a sympathetic smile.

'Korea was called the 'Hermit Kingdom' because of our centuries-long strict policy of limiting contact with the outside world. So little is known about our great country. We're glad foreigners like you can verify any false information.'

'It will take more than just me,' I responded.

'You're an excellent first step,' Mr Choe says, 'assuredly'.

I could feel Mr Song roll his eyes in exasperation, but that did not worry Choe, who smiled warmly.

* * *

North Korea is divided administratively into provinces, cities, counties, and the smallest unit, the village, called a *ri*. We entered Hoechang County. The dirt road followed a river, surrounded by mountains approximately 200 metres high, sufficient to block much of the sunlight.

Our convoy stopped in front of a large toolshed located along the river, named *Bongmyong*. This was the hydro-power installation which the County wanted to upgrade. Two large concrete tubes ran down the mountain to the shed to deliver water to a small power generator. We disembarked and approached the small shed. Inside, the two green tubes were silent. No sound of turbines generating any power. Against the wall a six-panel control board that looked really old, with small screens and dials and fuses. A barefoot man wearing mechanic blues was replacing black and red wires in a small wooden box by his feet. I spied an old rotary phone on a table by the panel. The whole set up looked barely functioning.

Mr. Song said that district officials were asking for Government support to upgrade the power plant. Outside the shed, I noticed a transformer that Choe said dated back to the time of cooperation with the Soviet Union. He peeked inside the shed, walked out, shaking his head in disappointment, saying, 'The District people made a huge effort to build a small dam, a reservoir uphill and a 1,370 metres long tunnel down the hill to bring water from the reservoir for this small hydro power station.' He turned to Song and I. 'All they have for power generation are these defective turbines. Their achievement is a waste of effort without bigger generators,' he concluded, in a sad tone.

As we returned to our car, Song looked at him sharply, his expression unreadable. Was he bristling at the suggestion that the people's efforts could be wasted? Or was he more concerned that Choe had spoken so

Figure 5.3 Soviet-era electrical capacitors. Their age makes them environmentally hazardous, as they leak PCBs into the soil and water. Photo by Jerome Sauvage.

freely in front of me? I had been in enough countries to recognize these occasions – the delicate balancing act between honesty and loyalty, between acknowledging hardship and upholding the official narrative. In this the North Koreans were not unusual, although I knew how cautious they had to be. One colleague mentioned to me that he attended self-criticism meetings on Saturday, during which every citizen individually confessed their shortcomings on the political loyalty front. The confessor then would hear additional criticism from others, then formed an action plan to compensate for those shortcomings. I had not expected to hear directly about the self-criticism sessions and I did not at the time think to ask for more details about them.

* * *

We drove along a paved road following the river between tall hills and entered the main County town, at the bottom of the valley. Under the low clouds, darkened by the hills, the town looked grey and joyless. Mr Choe provided geographical context on the County, detailing its location between plains and mountains. 'The District has 91,000 people, is mostly rural, with some small industry. There is a bit of water and sanitation work with UNICEF and one international NGO. The People's Committee is dynamic and wants to develop. We thought it would be a good place for UNDP to start something.'

We drove along official looking buildings, all in need of a coat of paint. A few people walked in the street but I could see no main street or market, no stores and I don't believe that a train line came here. The only colours to be seen appeared on murals and political slogans. One mural showed a woman in a yellow Korean traditional dress holding her son, a fat little boy, laughing and holding a textbook, standing in front of various products in jars and bottles, perhaps milk, sugar, and flour, a scale, an electric fan, and three pairs of shoes – one fine black pair for men, one white with heels for women, and rubber rain boots. To the woman's right, a graph with statistics and bars showed quantities produced, with exclamation points, as if to compensate for the empty shelves in stores. People walked by in black, blue or green outfit. Women's clothing often hung too wide at the shoulders and hips, for they were too thin. Young women sometimes arranged their hair into a ponytail

Figure 5.4 Mural, Hoechang City South Pyongyan Province. Photo by Jerome Sauvage.

held by a plastic clip. Men wore monochrome outfits with a vest that closed with a zipper and they sported a blue or black cap.

Our convoy entered a courtyard. This was the County People's Committee. The building, and the courtyard it surrounded, reminded me of a school, where classrooms opened onto an internal balcony overlooking the courtyard. A few men came out of the building to greet us. My UNDP colleague Mr Yu handled interpretation and introduced the Vice-Chairman of the People's Committee, Mr Han. He looked sturdy, his face deeply marked, receding black hair, and several front teeth repaired with a silver and greying alloy, the sight of which gave my own teeth a sensation of nerve pain. He wore the customary grey uniform with a breast pocket above which hung the lapel of Kim Il Sung and, inside the pocket, a pen. We shook hands; his was the hand of a working man.

* * *

The limited access to energy in North Korea had significantly hampered rural life, from pump irrigation to food transformation to access to safe drinking water. A UN household survey in 2005 among cooperative farms revealed that per capita energy consumption in rural areas amounted to half the national average. Cooking and heating in rural areas came largely from biomass fuel, a renewable energy source derived from organic materials like wood, agricultural residues and animal waste that could be burned directly or converted into liquid or gas fuels to generate heat or electricity.[1] They even used certain types of algae for energy! Coal and diesel oil and for a very small percentage (15 per cent), electricity from the grid provided the rest of energy consumed.

On the way to Haechong, we passed a truck running on biomass. It was one of those Chinese, green Army trucks, like in World War II movies. In the truck, young men in green uniforms sitting on the flatbed around a smoky steel drum were feeding straw, wood, corn residue and hay into the drum, out of which smoke escaped. Its speed was around 50 kms (35 miles) per hour. I first thought they were having a barbecue. It took me some time to realize that the drum was the truck's energy source. My first biomass-powered truck!

We walked to the upper floor, sat down, and then Vice-Chairman Han began, assisted by Yu, whose academic choice of words sounded stilted at times. Mr Han explained that the population of Haechong County was just under 100,000 persons, or 22,000 households; 90 hectares of rice fields (220 acres) for 62,000 hectares of forested area, mostly hills. They managed to clear 280 hectares (700 acres) for fruit

Figure 5.5 Biomass truck. Photo by Zharas Takenov.

trees. My colleague Yu quietly whispered to me that the fruit was also destined for export out of the DPRK. So much for feeding the people, I thought.

The only word I could use to describe energy usage in North Korea's rural areas is 'minuscule'. Almost nothing. The county only consumed 1,112 megawatts per hours, which equated to 12 kilowatts per households per year. Compare that to a US household that uses 1,000 times more energy!

It would be nearly impossible for the County to receive much electricity from the grid. The North Korean electricity grid was completely run down, struggling to recover ever since the 1990s, when cooperation with the Soviet Union ended. In the twenty-first century, North Korea's per capita energy use collapsed to one-third of what it was in the 1990s[2]. The average North Korean household used 271 kilograms of coal equivalent (kgCe) annually. In contrast, at the same time, US households consumed an annual average of 11,000 kilowatt-hours (kWh), equivalent to 1.3 tons of kgCe (2,600 lbs).[3]

Repairing North Korea's power system would require tens of billions of dollars in international cooperation. The issue extends beyond just energy production; the transmission infrastructure has not been maintained since the 1990s and would cost billions to repair. Although there are coal reserves in North Korea, the varying quality of coal and the lack of electricity needed for tasks such as lighting, operating jackhammers, moving coal, and pumping water out of flooded shafts are significant challenges. Energy insecurity was perhaps the biggest obstacle to North Korea's economic development.

The Vice-Chairman explained that his county's goal was to depend less on the grid by developing their own capacity and to keep whatever electricity they produced from hydro-power plants such as the one we had seen earlier in the day.

The County also extracted coal from a local mine. The coal was of poor quality, the mines partly flooded, the equipment was old and the work was 100 per cent manual due to lack of electricity. I shuddered at the thought of what work in a mine without electricity might look like or how high the rate of injuries and fatalities. Finally, we learned that the County received a little bit of oil from Government and from whatever the People's Committee could purchase. For cooking and heating and various energy-spending activities, Mr Han said, households used mostly biomass such as firewood or crop residues.

Yu continued in his flowery language, 'Although there is abundant wild fruit and edible plants in the mountains, local dwellers keep a small portion for family daily consumption,' he stated. 'The county aims to produce many processed foodstuff made of enriched wild fruit and wild herb to solve the food problem. In order to carry this out, it is important to raise the production capacity of our two factories decisively: Hoechang Wild Fruit Processing Factory and Basic Food Factory.' An important part of the solution, clearly, was to upgrade the two defective turbines I had seen earlier, at the hydropower installation at the bottom of the hill.

Listening to Yu, my mind drifted back to an old woman I had seen earlier, moving on the hill slope behind the hydropower shed we had stopped by. She was walking with painstaking slowness, her frail form bent permanently at the waist. A young boy, no older than eight, walked beside her, his small hand steadying her elbow. She picked through the underbrush, collecting tiny red fruits with a practiced precision that suggested a lifetime of doing just that. The pair evoked old engravings and ancient folktales, a sense of deep hardship, of absolute destitution. The weather had grown darker. I wondered if she had ever known a time when food was not something to be scavenged. The weight of their task, the quiet endurance in their movements, stayed with me long after we had moved on.

I returned to the conversation going on at the meeting.

'For the full use of this potential, it is necessary to upgrade our food processing factory at the *ri* level,' Han suggested.

Raising his head from his notebook, Choe asked all sorts of follow-up questions. 'How much wild food do you harvest every year? How do you extract sugar from corn? What is your factory capacity? What equipment upgrade is needed?'

Choe really wanted to understand the local economy. Vice Chairman Han: 'As I keep saying, our rural industry needs energy. With a little more energy, we can produce food locally: corn syrup, red chili paste . . . But for that, we must better equip the small hydropower station.[4] The power generators in Hoechang were not designed and manufactured according to the plants' specific characteristics but old ones that were left unused for a long time in other places. Inevitably the output is much lower than expected.'

I wonder how people perceived the fundamental unfairness of literally breaking their backs to build an infrastructure such as the hydro-power structure we had seen before entering town, only to not get the energy due to a lack of equipment. The more Choe engaged the county supervisor with questions and comments, the more Han and the local officials seemed to relax. Perhaps, they seemed to think, we will have our new turbines after all.

As for me, I was receiving good information on local conditions for local food and energy production. This was 'hard data' straight from the users and not from the MFA. By fielding a technical mission later on, we would be obtaining an accurate, undistorted picture of actual energy consumption in the county. It also became increasingly clear that a rehabilitation of those modest hydropower equipments was not only critical to solve nutritional challenges and agricultural production in Hoechang but also achievable within the scope of our projects. The infrastructure was in place, the dam built by the locals and conduits were in good shape. Our support would make a lot of difference to the county's population. I indicated that UNDP would need to run a socio-economic assessment before deciding how to invest in this local energy production. I was optimistic that the purchase of relatively small hydro-generators would receive sanctions exemptions from the US and UN authorities.

Just then, Mr Song started to speak. His voice started low, became more forceful after each pause for interpretation. 'Year of Juche 99 is a year of a general offensive in which we will concentrate all-Party nationwide efforts in the improvement of the people's living standards.

This past year, we successfully launched the artificial satellite Kwangmyo'ngso'ng-2 with our own technology, we successfully conducted a second underground nuclear test.'

I looked up around the table. Everyone kept a carefully inexpressive face, waiting. Such words had probably been heard many times by every Korean in the room.

'Remember the slogan of our great General Kim Jong Il: 'Let's achieve a decisive turnabout in people's living standards by accelerating light industry and agriculture once again!" Song continued. Everyone nodded automatically. Now he turned towards the Vice-Chairman.

'The industrial sector should positively push ahead with the renovation of hydroelectric power plants. All power capacity should support the construction of the great State!'

I was not sure what Mr Song was after. Did he imply that the Centre had priority over County-level as regards energy upgrades, or did he simply remind the County that they depended upon the central Government for improvement in their infrastructure? In any case, everyone, even Mr Choe, was looking at their hands folded on the table, their faces careful not to betray emotion. The Vice-Chairman looked worried. I wondered, how complicated was this going to be?

* * *

We visited the Hoechang Wild Fruit Processing Factory and the Basic Food Factory that transform wild fruit and other plants that people collect from the mountains. Inside the large, bare room, a dozen workers in plastic boots and chef hats busied themselves near a Chinese-made oven. In another corner, a steam engine powered an antique biscuit maker. On the other side of the room, an equally old mill separated buds of maize and produced molasses syrup. All of it Chinese equipment, dating back to the 1970s.

On a table, samples of fruit and vegetables were exposed. I saw acorn, which makes jam and a sweet jelly; wild grape and wild pear, to prepare syrup. A flat oblong reddish pod, tara, contained a few large round black seeds used as stabilizer in sauces, as thickener in dairy products and as emulsifier. Although these machines were functioning, it seemed like only samples were being produced for our viewing. The production line was not robust and the factory had a disused air. The County manager noticed my reaction and said, 'Without energy, we do not use the line enough.'

In Hoechang, local people collected 800 tons of wild fruit and 180 tons of wild herbs per year, 850 tons of fruit and 4,300 tons of vegetables.

They transformed less than half of the food collected into food products like jam etc.

'How do they manage to keep such antique equipment going?' I asked Choe.

'We are excellent engineers, technicians, repairmen.' Choe thought, then smiled.

'Were you going to say something more, Mr Choe?'

'I was reflecting on the traditional criticism from the outside world that if we are good engineers and repairmen, then we cannot also be ground-breaking inventors of new technologies.'

'Is that so? Are you?'

'I hope that you will see during your stay some of our notable achievements and the solutions that we have found with very little resources!'

Pointing at the whole place, I asked, 'Is this where they produce all the food for the *ri*?'

'This is one of the main factories,' Choe replied, 'and by far not enough for a hundred thousand people.'

'When do they gather the plants?' I asked.

'In North Korea, workplaces and factories let their people leave during the day to forage in the hills. The cold season is long in North Korea. It's a matter of survival. The people get to keep some and bring the rest to the factory,' explained Choe. Later on, I checked with members of the DPRK MFA whether it was a policy to allow people to leave work in order to forage for food. They confirmed it[5].

Mr. Choe pulled me by the arm and pointed, as if this were a good joke, at an old tin, marked 'Gift of the people of the USA.' It was now being used to contain machine oil.

Mr. Han picked a small round bready piece rolling down a cooling conveyor belt.

'Kids in school like these biscuits but they have little nutrient value. I wish we could make better use of the fruit we have in the hills.'

Han paused.

'We just need to produce more energy.'

It was painfully clear: without significant investment in energy, the North Korean people would remain trapped in destitution. The regime ensured that electricity was supplied to the elites, the military, and the mechanisms of control. However, in places like Hoechang, people lived in darkness, forced to improvise and endure. I thought about Mr Han's quiet frustration, Choe's careful questions, and the old woman in the woods. What I had seen were not just statistics in an energy

Figure 5.6 Food production equipment, Hoechang City, South Pyongyan Province. Note the food can, a gift of the US, used as an oil container. Photo by Jerome Sauvage.

report – these were lives, confined and shaped by forces beyond their control. As I sat at that table, I recognized that even our best efforts here would face limitations: how much could we achieve before confronting the boundaries of what was possible?

* * *

We crossed a courtyard and entered a small building where, in a cold, drab square room without glass on the windows and with only a table for furniture, a few men awaited us, dressed in dark blue or grey trousers, padded jackets and white shirts, each with a pen in their shirt breast pockets. The table was on the floor and covered in small dishes with, at its centre, a hot coal plate. Han gestured to Song, Choe and I to sit down while some others joined and some left the room. I struggled a bit to sit with my legs to one side tucked under.

'These are all roots from our country,' Choe said, gesturing at the table.

Han named the dishes: 'Konchi, Totori, Taade … we soak them overnight.' He pointed at twigs in a bunch, each a thin thread with dark fruit like small olives, dark green, red, or yellow, cooked inside a dark sweet sauce.

Even before going to Korea, I had always loved Korean food. But some of these roots were new to me. I wrote down their names in a notebook. Some, I never found again outside of the DPRK. Some roots felt sweet and others, like pungi, tasted like anise. There was also kimchi and other pickled vegetables as well as beer. The whole time, Han and the others listed the food's therapeutic benefits.

'In Korean food, you balance the body energies with five elements: The fire element is bitter, good for the heart and small intestine; wood is sour, for liver and gallbladder; water is salty, for kidneys and bladder; metal is spicy, for lungs and large intestines, and earth is sweet, good for the stomach and pancreas!'

Young Mr Yu became animated as he translated each human body organ accurately. I had heard this from my Asian in-laws and friends: 'Balance in food is everything,' they used to say.

Mr. Han saw how much I was enjoying this, so he went on . . . 'Balance and harmony! These things accompany Korean food: The first is respect, the second is balance and harmony, and the third is health.'

Han pointed at a pile of grey roots. 'Toraji, a cousin of ginseng, bellflower with long roots.' Showing the ginseng, someone made a joke in Korean, others laughed loudly, and I assumed the joke was sexual in nature. Choe tried to translate it for me: 'If a man or a woman takes ginseng, the other will feel it. If they both take ginseng, the bed will feel it.'

Mr Choe, who had no appetite, lit a cigarette and turned towards me.

'I see you like it? Korea is the paradise of fermentation.' I told him what I read once on a Brooklyn brewery's wall: 'Fermentation is the basis of civilization.' He laughed and translated it to Korean, making everyone chuckle around the table.

Chapter 6

COUNTING SOULS

A first look at the humanitarian situation – The first population census in ten years

Early weeks in January proved especially busy for North Koreans, when Kim Jong Il's traditional January directives were published in the form of an annual New Year Editorial in the Party newspaper *Rodong Sinmun* and the Korean People's Army Daily *Joson Inmingun*. These directives, presented by the Leader at major WPK meetings, outlined advancements and challenges in various sectors (political, economic, military, etc.) and set targets for the coming year. Enterprises shut down in anticipation for new directives. Large amounts of time was spent in January to learn and memorize, then February was dedicated to planning and budgeting. North Koreans abroad were traditionally called back to recount the previous year, especially financially. Our office did receive a copy in English. I tried to read the editorial and did my best to find anything useful. Amid the 6,000 words, I found the word 'should' 95 times, 'great' 70 times and 'battle' 21 times. At least, light industry and agriculture were presented as the focus for the 'struggle for improving the people's living standards' and organic farming was mentioned. Beyond that, four areas were required for national investment towards people's living standards: provision of raw materials and materials needed for light industrial goods production; 'economic construction'; expanding foreign markets and trade. The editorial did not explain how these goals would be achieved. On energy, Mr Song was right: the directives recommend the construction of large-scale hydroelectric power plants. Not a word on micro or renewable energy. Politically, the word 'reunification' was used twenty-one times, which, at the time, seemed like a positive and a nod to the South for the year ahead.

* * *

At the beginning of my first full year in the DPRK, in his hand-over to me, departing WFP Rep and Coordinator Mads had listed 3 major obstacles in delivering a programme in the DPRK with which I would be struggling for my entire stay in the DPRK: poor infrastructure, difficulty enforcing monitoring, and a near-total absence of statistics and figures. That last problem had a major impact on our work. Development and humanitarian work relied on numbers – infant mortality rates, food security indices, economic indicators. Without them, how were we supposed to plan? I had anticipated obstacles – bureaucratic hurdles, funding shortfalls – but this was the crux of where UN expectations of transparency and information as fundamental to solving problems and designing programmes hit the wall of North Korea's penchant for secrecy and control. This underlying contradiction between our work and the DPRK environment would deeply inform so much about what and how we could operate. As a first step in what I thought was the right direction, we quickly endorsed FAO and WFP's recommendation to organize a comprehensive food assessment for the year 2010, at the end of the Fall harvest. This would get us some real, timely and valuable information about the food situation.

I soon discovered that the UN had decisively addressed the damning lack of data from and about the DPRK when I helped the UNFPA roll out their 2008 Population Census.

The fact that the 2008 Census happened at all was nothing short of a miraculous feat. In 'North Korea: State of Paranoia,' Paul French points out that, 'Essentially no reliable statistics have been published by the DPRK since 1965.'[1] For the rest of my mission, I was astonished by the DPRK's inability or unwillingness to collect, use and publish data when it could coerce its citizenry to do many other non-productive things. The causes for such scarcity of statistics were multiple. To be sure, the office in charge of statistics, the Central Bureau of Statistics (CBS) lacked capacity. This seemed surprising since the CBS had been established in the 1950s and placed under the State Planning Commission, itself under the Cabinet, the supreme administrative organ of North Korea, directly under the Leader. But in my years there, the CBS' capacity was never close to that of any other country I knew of.

The DPRK's stunning lack of transparency in statistics had existed ever since Kim Il Sung is said to have declared all statistics subject to national security. As an academic observer once wrote: '*Normal countries publish figures. Even less than normal countries manage a few. The numbers may be lousy, or indeed lies, but this is what states do … Therefore, when the DPRK Central Statistics Bureau starts doing its job in public, then (and only then) will we know that reform in North Korea is for real and irreversible*.'[2] This lack of transparency came from a culture of fear that permeated every level, down to the smallest administrative unit. It brought to mind the excesses of the Great Leap Forward in China in the late 1950s to early 1960s, when Chinese officials frequently fabricated statistics, particularly regarding agricultural output. This was often done to meet unrealistic goals set by Mao, leading to widespread data falsification and, ultimately, famine. During my travels through North Korea's provinces, I talked to heads of Provincial Departments for health or agriculture who truly and sincerely did not know their annual budget, and to doctors in local maternity wards who reported without evidence that their district had not experienced a single maternal death for the past year.

A third cause for the lack of data was that each Government Ministry, Agency or Bureau was very siloed. Gathering quality figures involves an upward movement from the bottom to the top where data is gathered and also a transversal effort as no single piece of information belongs exclusively to one source. The Central Bureau of Statistics in this case experienced the difficulties of any office across the world that needs to cut across vertical Government agencies in order to obtain reliable information.

I recalled how UNDP had supported, in the area of statistics, Vietnam's transition from a centrally planned economy to a socialist-oriented market economy. I could tell that in the DPRK we were a long way from reproducing such a feat. In the 1980s UNDP assisted Vietnam in refining data collection methods, ensuring that it was accurate and reliable, helped improve analysis and supported the dissemination of statistical information to the public and other stakeholders. This work fostered transparency and accountability. UNDP also played a role in integrating Vietnam's statistical system with international standards and practices, making it more comparable with other economies, facilitating international collaboration and attracting foreign investment. North Korea was not prepared to match such standards.

Whatever the reasons, the absence of reliable data would force us and all other development and humanitarian organizations to spend precious resources whenever starting a new project. We gathered figures and facts from scratch and ensured that every statistic we published emanated from our own assessments and verifications.[3]

This time around, international experts who evaluated the 2008 Census after its release confirmed that its overall quality was far superior to the first census ever completed in 1993, when it was beset by a lack of experience and in the midst of a famine.[4]

The 2008 census partially owed its existence to South Korea's 'Sunshine Policy', mentioned earlier. During this period, the UN secured a commitment from South Korea and Switzerland to fund the census, which continued undeterred by new inter-Korean difficulties.

To accomplish this immense task, the UNFPA hired one of their top specialists on population statistics in Asia, who will be named Christina here. Christina had already fought census battles in the region and was uniquely qualified for this one. She and the whole team in the region had carefully trained North Korean counterparts in collecting and analysing the collected information, an essential step to ensure safety, respect and avoid misuse of the process. Population surveying and registering knew a dark history in the DPRK. In the 1960s and 70s, North Korea conducted a census of sorts called *Songbun*, the Resident Registration Project of 1967–1970, which placed the entire population into three main classifications: the core class of loyal cadres; the 'wavering class', which was suspect and monitored; and the 'hostile class', which was politically unreliable and about 50 sub-classifications based on family background and performance in political tests, among other criteria. People obtained or were denied jobs, granted access to the Party or housing on the basis of those classifications. This time, the census strictly followed the highest international standards.

The census taught us many important facts about the North Korean population. There were 24 million North Koreans in 2008, but population growth was slow. The 1990s famine had significantly impacted the country's age pyramid. There was a visible 'dent' in the younger population, reflecting the sharp decline in births during that period and resulting in a smaller population of young adults compared to older generations.[5]

People lived in households, usually a family that stayed together and shared a common arrangement for food. This matters in North Korea: the regime has never quite managed to break the family, that most persistent collection of individuals, and the census reflected it. Whereas observers wrote that 'the most valued and exclusive human connection in North Korean society is that between individuals (each isolated and in separation from the other) and the sovereign Leader',[6] statistics stubbornly showed that almost everyone belonged to a household. As a result, UN statisticians chose the household as the core social unit, through which every person in the country was enumerated. They had to mention exceptions, however: those living in institutional or collective living quarters such as dormitories, orphanages, and prison camps or in military camps, which were also counted.

North Korea appeared clearly as a patriarchal society, with men invariably considered heads of households. State policy on housing also influenced the formation of households. When a young couple married, they were provided with a separate housing unit, thus enabling them to establish a household of their own. However, when housing units were not readily available, newly married couples continued to live with the husband's family for several years after marriage, giving rise to extended households. Results from the census revealed that the majority of households (64 per cent) were still of the nuclear type while extended households comprised nearly a third of the total.[7]

As various authors noted, '*The war-induced necessity of rapidly rebuilding Pyongyang, and the political policy of resettling many rural people in cities and towns, have given North Korea a relatively high population density of approximately 185,000 people per square kilometre – similar to Italy or Switzerland*.'[8] However the census indicated that the rate of urbanization may have slowed, because no one could move from one place to another (and certainly not to Pyongyang) without authorization. Slower urbanization could also be attributed to the country's policy to maintain a population balance in all regions in the country and notably, to keep workers for agricultural work in rural areas.

The census was clear: the North Korean population was ageing, and fast. Fertility in the North followed the same declining pattern as in its southern neighbour. Beginning in the late seventies, the fertility rate had begun to decline following programmes designed to improve the health of children and women while increasing women's participation in the workplace. The number of births continued to increase because of the increased population born during the post-war pro-natalist era when the regime tried to compensate for the loss of lives reaching reproductive age. It was not until the mid-nineties that reduced fertility rates resulted in a decline in the number of babies born.

The census' filled me with a sense of possibility. The UN had been able to produce and distribute worldwide a trove of information about the DPRK. The UNFPA had managed to convince the Government to release a regular, baseline census at acceptable international standards. The project brought the two Koreas together despite their difficult relationship. Switzerland helped in critical ways beyond funding. The Representative, one of the most experienced specialists on the DPRK, lent her credibility to help convince all the parties to collaborate. I was eager to find out if we could deliver equally good information on the state of North Korea's food production and consumption. The task would prove as difficult as it was important.

Chapter 7

ECONOMY OF HUNGER

Crop and Food Security Assessment Mission – A conversation – The Public Distribution System and markets – A cooperative farm – UN expert on economics and politics of food

In the DPRK, decisions relating to food, including its production and distribution – as well as State budget allocation and the use of international aid – are ultimately made by a small group of officials, who are not accountable to the people affected by their decisions. In 2014, the UN General Assembly's Human Rights Commission ordered a commission of inquiry on human rights in the DPRK, led by Justice Kirby of Australia.[1] Regarding food, the report recommended that the DPRK ensure that citizens enjoy the right to food without discrimination; pay particular attention to the needs of women and vulnerable groups, such as street children, the elderly and persons with disabilities; promote agricultural, economic and financial policies based on democratic participation; and legalize and support free market activities and other independent economic conduct that provide citizens with a livelihood.

The report also advocated that outside countries should not use the provision of food and other essential humanitarian assistance to impose economic or political pressure on the DPRK. Aid should only be curbed to the extent that unimpeded international humanitarian access and related monitoring is not adequately guaranteed. Bilateral and multilateral providers of assistance should coordinate their efforts to ensure that adequate conditions of humanitarian access and related monitoring are provided by the DPRK Government. This human-rights based approach to aid was an important articulation of principles, yet challenging to adhere to in real-life implementation.

* * *

The 2010 harvest was completed and the weather dry and cool. Now we could obtain and share with the world a more exact evaluation of the country's agriculture and nutritional conditions, in the form of a Crop and Food Security Assessment Mission (CFSAM) report. There was some anticipation among us as we'd had an assessment in 2004 and in 2008 but somehow not in 2009. The Crop and Food Security Assessment is a tool that is used by FAO and WFP for developing countries that are highly dependent on agriculture (a massive 23 per cent of the local population are employed in agriculture in North Korea). The assessment evaluates the production of winter and spring crops, and estimates cereal import requirements for the coming year, including food assistance needs. It provides essential data to project the agriculture sector's contribution to the economy, as well as how to plan for the coming season. But most importantly for the DPRK, it would give us a view of the food supply available to the North Korean people for the year ahead.

To arrange for that assessment, FAO and WFP negotiated every step, and the North Koreans conceded as little terrain as possible. Of the country's ten provinces, it was finally agreed, the Mission would visit seven that normally account for about 90 per cent of the nation's cereal production: North Pyongan, South Pyongan, North Hwanghae, South Hwanghae, North Hamgyong, South Hamgyong and Kangwon. They would triangulate official crop area and production figures with their interviews with Government and cooperative-farm officials, and through their direct observation of standing and harvested crops. Government-supplied information would be analysed with international weather records as well as independent satellite photos of crop areas from the European Union's geophysical analysis services. The Mission also would visit rural and urban households in all the selected provinces, schools, nurseries, hospitals, public distribution centres (PDCs) and some county grain storage facilities.

I was disappointed to learn that the mission would gain only limited access into state shops or open markets.[2] Such access was normal for any food assessment mission anywhere else in the world. Limited access to state shops or open markets would make it more difficult to assess the variety of commodities sold or incomes earned from these activities. Another limitation were interviews into households, used to classify them by their food security status on the basis of their rations of cereals. Without reliable information on wages and income sources by various socio-economic groups, it would be difficult to understand the extent to which various households had access to other foods over-and-above cereals.

When the concerned organizations decided to go ahead despite the limitations, it proved to be a good decision: they collected plenty of information, establishing a baseline for subsequent assessments; the following year, the 2011 mission did obtain complete access to markets and was able to interview households[3]. Bilateral countries and other multilateral organizations joined in this unique opportunity to take an in-depth look at the country, outside of Pyongyang. Representatives from Australia and the European Union travelled to North Korea to join the mission. There'd be plenty to see and report back to their respective Governments. I would join two visiting participants on their first stage to Wonsan, the city to the east. I will name these fictional mission members: 'Tripathy', UN FAO's Food and Nutrition specialist and 'Michael', who followed developments in the DPRK from a Western Embassy in Beijing. This mission offers a unique opportunity for any diplomat to see in person the situation in the country. Most food assessments missions I have seen during my tenure have accommodated representatives from individual countries or international organizations such as the European Union, who took advantage of the rare access these UN missions provided.

In Pyongyang the team met with non-governmental and bilateral agencies working in DPRK: the experienced head of the Swiss Development Cooperation; the Red Cross; development agencies from Italy, Sweden, the European Union. With any luck, some visiting representatives from non-resident agencies and NGOs would be here.

I was able to observe more closely than in any previous posts how NGOs operated. There were as many operating styles as there were organizations. One difference consisted in which ones resided in North Korea versus those that did not. Six NGOs were established in Pyongyang: two from France, and one each from Belgium, Germany, Ireland and the United Kingdom. They functioned under the sponsorship of the Europe Union's Aid Cooperation Office, which was not an official European Aid branch, but still could offer funding and some protection against excessive Government requirements or pressure. In addition, the Swiss Agency for Development and Cooperation, the Italian Development Cooperation Office, a Swedish Agricultural Rehabilitation Project, and the International Federation of Red Cross and Red Crescent Societies, also operated in the country. The UN and the NGOs each depended upon a different office inside the MFA. As a result, the Government discouraged cooperation between UN and NGOs, which we would try and resist through our own coordination meetings, thematic groups and occasional joint activities.[4]

Non-resident NGOs visited regularly and among them, organizations from the US: Christian NGOs with decades-long history of cooperation in Northeast Asia or specifically the DPRK, and with deep experience and knowledge: Quakers, American-Canadian Mennonites and other Christian NGOs such as Christian Friends of Korea and World Vision. I learned that a few months before my arrival, five American NGOs had been asked to leave North Korea, showing how tenuous their hold in-country could be.

Programmes from these agencies offered a wide range of discrete interventions from agricultural development to heath and sanitation, disability and even some institution-building. They provided training and study tours abroad and just like us in the UN, they experienced the challenges of explaining their work, defending any kind of long-term development over mere humanitarian aid and negotiated tirelessly with the DPRK authorities over securing working conditions meeting international standards.

The NGOs, international agencies such as the Red Cross and bilateral programmes experienced uniquely difficult working conditions. They also proved remarkably impactful because they came to the DPRK when so few others would, and they worked as directly as possible with the North Korean people. I hope someone will soon write their stories, for they are rich in human interaction and important lessons.

* * *

The road to Wonsan is the only highway to the east coast, better than the compacted dirt road that I had taken to Haechong on my first field trip. Mr Pak drove the car smoothly along a well-designed highway, cruising through a striking landscape of mountains, waterfalls, and trees hanging over precipices. Our path climbed steadily from Pyongyang up into the mountain ranges that ran the length of North Korea's east coast, reminding me of vertical Chinese landscape paintings with jagged cliffs among hills covered in shades of green foliage. In the late autumn weather, gingko trees splashed bright gold amidst the evergreen oaks, conifers, and red maples. We moved fast on an empty road and through tunnel after unlit tunnel.

The daylight gradually dimmed as we climbed higher across ever more inhospitable terrain. When we entered Sinphyong County, in North Hwangae Province, spikes towered high above the road, their bristly edges lacerating misty clouds that floated up from the sea like the fingers of ghosts. Shapes out of this world appeared and disappeared through fog. A tree grew askew from the cliff shards, three flat stones seeking stable ground. The harsh but beautiful scenery felt like a metaphor: maybe I could pass through this muddle of rock and fog and emerge, safe, on the other side.

Wonsan City lays down lazily on the east coast along what North Koreans call the East Sea. Near the hotel, there was a promenade over the beach. Behind the hotel, a jetty projected out into the bay, ending with a small lighthouse. Hotel Dongmyong, far from a Riviera-esque site, emphasized functionality with large concrete blocks and a minimalist aesthetic. You could see from the outside the purpose of each room: dining tables at floor level, beds on floors above. It was painted with that unmistakable institutional Army green, becoming familiar to me. Inside, the atrium lobby rose to the fifth floor, with inner balconies facing each other.

The hotel management informed us that there would be water available between five and seven p.m., so some of us decided to take a walk to the end of the pier. Tripathy, Michael and I met downstairs. Of the North Koreans, only the representative from the Ministry of Agriculture, a Mr An, showed up. We stepped onto the pier and took in the fresh sea air smelling of the black and green seaweed covering nearby rocks jutting out of the sand. To our right on a small jetty, a dozen men tried their chance at fishing, their bicycles parked near them, and a woman with a large circular net combed the water a few feet off the beach. Michael and Tripathy took off on a brisk walk, and soon Mr An and I lagged behind. For a brief passage of time we were alone looking at the shore and the people on the pier.

Mr. An seemed to relax, enjoying the ocean air. I started a conversation.

'Your country is unlike any I've ever seen.'

'We are an exception, and we know it.'

'How so?'

'For one, we are a unique people.'

I sensed an opening and tried my chance.

'The Korean people, indeed, are exceptional,' I began 'Unfortunately, they are a divided people.'

He shook his head.

'Only the DPRK keeps the Korean people exceptional.'

'Aren't they just as exceptional in the South?'

An answered, 'our people are pure.'

Surprised by his tone, I slowed my pace, but Mr An pushed my elbow lightly and we walked again. I remembered that we should not appear engaged in serious conversation. I had already heard of the rhetoric of 'pure race'. Mr An revealed a worldview that was not just nationalistic but ethno-nationalist in nature. The year we had this conversation, author B.R Myers published *The Cleanest Race*,[5] analysing racial purity themes in the DPRK's propaganda. The author describes how North Korea's Government did not base its ideology on Marxism–Leninism or

Neo-Confucianism, but on Imperial Japan fascism. The regime's racist criteria for national identity painted its 'genetically pure' Korean citizens as innocent and morally virtuous but militarily weak, requiring the Leader's charismatic guidance and protection. I wondered whether Mr An's exposure to foreigners of all hues and races could broaden his worldview, if one day a more accurate dialogue about identity, ideology and the weight of history would ever be possible in the country.

Political conversations with North Koreans were rare and I found them difficult to navigate. I once spoke with another interlocutor about the West, in a conversation that went something like this: 'In the United States also, there used to be racial discrimination,' I started. 'Black people were prevented from integrating housing or schools, were denied jobs based on race and forbidden to inter-marry, even in the mid-twentieth century. But things changed for the better.'

'Westerners always ask us that question: can you change?' my interlocutor answered. You think that we will open up like a nice flower ready to be plucked?'

'Do you want to change?'

'We want progress, but we know who we are. We know more about the West than you think we do: you may call yourselves free, but we see that not everyone is in the same boat. You have inequality, homelessness, violence, racism … We watch the news, you know!'

'True,' I conceded, 'but we can work for things to change.'

'Change for what?' he insisted.

'Change for better life conditions, more comfort, equality, happiness.' I answered vaguely.

'Comfort . . . Our bellies may not be full and our lives may be hard, but we lead a life that is bigger than ourselves.'

The conversation left me with a mixed sense of frustration and fascination. It was the first time that I had heard the worshipful fervour associated with North Korean official ideology, which I had read about.[6] Did history shape this worldview or was it just isolation? In either case, the result seemed to reinforce fear of the outside.

* * *

At breakfast, the sky was clear and the sun was shining. I counted the exact number of plates laid out in advance over large round tables. Our group of foreigners sat at one table, the North Koreans at another. Another visiting Delegation, westerners also, ate silently at a third table. Otherwise, we were alone in this huge hotel. Tripathy was speaking with Michael, and I joined them.

Tripathy was discussing Juche, the North Korean doctrine of self-reliance. 'North Korea upholds a myth. Food-wise, self-reliance is a myth. They have nature against them; 80 per cent of the land is mountainous . . .'

'I don't know . . . perhaps they can reach self-sufficiency. At least in cereal production,' said Michael. 'You can grow food on the slopes.'

'You cannot grow cereal crops on the slopes. And with winters lasting as long as Minnesota or Norway, you need a lot more input to achieve more than one cereal crop per year. Plus, they have these typhoons.'

'You are describing Japan, and Japan is doing it pretty well,' the diplomat attested with optimism.

'Come on, Michael! Even with fertilizers, seeds, and technology, Japan is not food self-sufficient.'

'Because they're not trying to be. They trade and agriculture is a small part of their economy.'

Tripathy passed his hands over his face. 'As I said, North Korea says it is aiming at self-sufficiency. Today, we'll find out how it's working.'

We climbed into one car, so we could exchange our impressions and speak a little more privately, even in the presence of Pak, our driver. 'You will not have a lot of time to see everything,' Tripathy warned us. 'They've arranged these visits because we insisted. They always tried to limit the time, the scope of what we'll see. We will spend but a few precious minutes at each site. So, you two, use your experience to take things in and to look past what is being presented to you . . .'

I learned over time to develop the ability of 'looking behind the Potemkin Village' as Tripathy demanded of us. A 'Potemkin village' has become a metaphor for a deceptive façade, or a false appearance created to hide an underlying reality of suffering, poverty, or inadequacy. It is named after the Russian prince Potemkin who is said to have ordered the construction of fake villages to deceive Empress Catherine the Great.

As observers we needed to be aware of our hosts' attempts at manipulation, concealment or a false sense of prosperity. We needed to use common sense. To assess if a place has energy, do you see electric wires coming into a building? In the fields, are there tractors or ploughs during harvest? For the rest, you have to ask questions, triangulate answers and not take anything at face value.

We visited a Public Distribution Center in Wonsan. It was a bare room at the foot of a five-story apartment building, the paint peeling off the walls. On one side of the room, officials sat behind a counter with a large registry book in front of them. In a corner of the room Tripathy pointed at a tall concrete container, with a pipe and a dispenser at waist level.

'The system distributes oils, sugar, and all sorts of cereals – corn, rice, barley, but one type at a time, depending on supply.'

The distribution centre was quiet. The short line outside was orderly and there was no confusion inside. Women and men entered the room one by one, holding an ID card and an empty sack, marked a pause when they saw us, unsure about our presence. They walked to the counter and showed their ID.

'*This is the type of place where millions of North Koreans get their staple food*,' I thought. Having their identity established, each individual stood in front of the dispenser, extended their sack under the stopper, and let the cereal fall into the bag.

'They're supposed to get two cups of cereal per family member each day,' Tripathy said, pointing at a woman receiving her rations. 'The normal target ration is 570 grams of cereal per day per person (1.2 lbs). For over a decade now, these targets have never been reached. Currently, on average, households get 370 grams of mixed cereal commodities (0.82 lbs), or 50 per cent of their daily energy requirement.'[7]

The woman who had her sack filled looked inside and shook it a little. She seemed to figure out whether this would be enough to feed her family before the next distribution.

I was very uncomfortable watching this scene. This was no longer a food system based on the idea of the State ensuring for everyone their fair share of food. The control element was evident. The history of famine loomed large. People were aware of food, and hunger. How could they rise to change their condition, so tied to the State's food rations and the system behind it?

Meanwhile Tripathy continued his explanations. 'Besides these cereal rations,' he said, 'Koreans buy salt, bean-paste, soy sauce, oil and vegetables from state shops where prices are controlled. Availability and variety in those shops vary and are not reliable sources for everyone. You also have the private farmers markets.'

We drove to another part of the town and entered a covered market, or a 'general market'. It was a concrete covered structure like a hangar, with limited and guarded entry points. Booths were built in concrete and wood and each had a number. Women worked the stalls, wearing different coloured uniforms with numbers on their lapel. Again, Tripathy emphasized the problem with markets. 'In these markets, called *Jangmadang*, people may find mostly fruit and vegetables. Market prices! Sometimes the authorities close the market . . .' He did not elaborate. This market in Wonsan carried a greater variety of items than I had seen in Pyongyang: small tools, socks, some school supplies. I did not see any rice being sold in the market, although I heard about a black market for rice. It was good to see vegetables and fruit lying around, healthy-looking cabbage, greens, a few apples . . .

'No photos!' one of our handlers said nervously, placing his hand on my arm. The place looked like a market anywhere else around the world but for the relatively lower noise and a certain amount of tension. I felt that anxiety in the eyes of women crouching on their heels amid the booths, heightened by the presence of police. The lack of trust between seller and buyer was visible. Some customers brought their own scale to accurately weigh their purchases, Individuals walked along aisles to sell sugar on the sly. And yet, as one international observer mentioned around the time of my visit, 'markets seemed to provide one of the least constrained environments for the exchange of news, information, and rumour',[8] and this was also true. After perhaps twenty minutes, our handlers rushed us back in the car. Frustrated by the incomplete visit, I started to pepper Tripathy with questions.

'You said that sometimes the authorities close the market . . .'

'The authorities tolerate the *Jangmadang* because they don't have a choice. Markets began after the famine, and they never could do without them. They tried again last November, but as you can see the markets are back.' Tripathy answered. 'They need markets, but their existence challenges the narrative of an all-providing State. The Leader doesn't want them. Market days and hours are limited. They are tolerated, but not encouraged.'

'Why don't they sell cereals at the market?' I asked.

'Government doesn't want rice prices to rise, and cereals are the last vestige of Government control via the Public Distribution System. The PDS is also the last remnant of the ideal society without money, where food is distributed for free. Today, people with money can find rice in clandestine ways. You will see, on the street, people exchanging things . . . People sell or barter goods and services like sewing, small trading, shoe or bicycle repair.'

'Bartering? Didn't know it still existed,' said Michael.

'The current rate for meat is two pounds of pork for 4.5 pounds of rice. But the rate changes all the time,' Tripathy continued. 'You have to be in the heart of that economy to know every variation.'

I had heard in Pyongyang that a woman provided make-up sessions for brides and special occasions, to either earn money or barter, a sign of entrepreneurship.

'So there is money around?'

'The average income per family is estimated to be about NKW3,000 to NKW5,000 per month. On the black market, that amount fluctuates around USD5 per month!'[9] Tripathy answered.

'These women look like they run the market,' I remarked.

'In my estimation, women saved North Korea after the famine of the mid-1990s,' Tripathy answered. 'The Public Distribution System collapsed. There was hunger, then a famine. Women came to understand how little to expect from the State and to protect their families they re-discovered their own resourcefulness. The markets have been a fixture ever since. In a way, that is when the institution of the family defeated the regime's attempt to replace it.'

I tried to imagine what the power of women meant in private markets, given their relatively low status in North Korean society. It could be a real threat. The regime had tried to quell the emerging cash-wielding, self-supporting traders during the previous year's currency re-denomination. The population had to turn in their old *won* bills for new ones, but with a cap of NKW100,000 per family, anyone with any excess amount would receive 1 new *won* for 100 old *won*, thus basically wiping out much of the private savings and wealth.[10] Overnight every shop and market closed. The currency devalued and everyone holding

Figure 7.1 Roadside vendors, South Pyongan Province, Nampo, South Pyongan Province. Courtesy of Eric Lafforgue.

cash found themselves holding one per cent of the original value. Just like that.

* * *

On the way to a cooperative farm, Tripathy gave us some context:

> North Korean cooperative farms were established under Kim Il Sung's leadership in the 1950s, and have remained the backbone of the country's collectivized agricultural system. They replaced private land ownership with collective labour. Typically, a cooperative farm consists of multiple small villages working together under Government supervision, with farmers assigned plots that they do not personally own. All production belongs to the state, which distributes food according to national planning. However, in practice, farmers struggle to meet quotas. Since the 1990s famine, some farms have allowed limited private plots, providing a modest incentive for higher yields and a safety valve for families.

Tripathy finished just as we entered a valley, dotted with farm buildings. The farm was about three miles long by one-and-a-half wide, bordered by hills. Not a tree to be seen on that valley floor: every parcel of land was dedicated to farming. No heavy equipment like a tractor or a combine in sight either. Some fields were recently harvested. Some had the crop of corn still lying on the ground, unpicked.

We entered the Cooperative Farm. White, low-slung buildings surrounded a large square yard, neat, and bare, looking like a small factory. Covered hangars held threshing machines and piles of corn perhaps three feet high, already husked, laid on the floor. A woman of about forty years stepped forward. She was the farm manager, dressed in military pants and suit jacket with six dark brassy buttons and a Mao collar; she wore blue Chinese tennis shoes. On her lapel, a small round pin of Kim Il Sung. Her hair was parted on the left side and tied in the back, with a few wisps straying over her forehead. Always a little startling, the red lipstick contrasted with the military green ensemble. Her attentiveness to everything, quietly ordering her deputy who obeyed while pretending not to, the way she greeted everyone, left no mistake that she was the boss.

'There are 600 families on the farm,' she said. 'A foreign NGO helped us make a pond where we keep fish, we appreciated that.' She went on, repeating herself, 'But other than that time, we rely on ourselves.'

We walked over to the pond. It was 200 square metres. Inside, fish that looked like carps and minnows could be seen. They must have represented a good source of food, albeit limited considering that the farm population would be between 1,500 and 2,000 people. 'That pond is also used for learning,' the manager said, enumerating all her new knowledge. 'Filtration, water oxygenation, fish species . . .' She smiled as she seemed to remember the steps they went through. 'One NGO and an American university in New York State shared many useful resources!'

She proudly gestured towards a dozen roofs, including one atop a small dispensary, where a wind turbine whirred quietly. 'We hope to buy small rotors ourselves once trade with China eases up. Some of us even make our own blades. All we need is the generator.' This pond and these small wind turbines spelled 'self-sufficiency' at the local level. The manager's demeanour reminded me of Vice Chair Han, Haechong County's executive: these managers ran the show, didn't expect much from the capital city and focused on making their community work a little better. Michael walked behind me, smiling, and whispered, '*The mountains are high and the Emperor is far away*,' repeating this traditional Chinese saying alluding *to local officials' tendency to disregard the wishes of central authorities* in the distant capital city.

* * *

We sat inside a home on the farm. This visit was allowed in order to give the team some context. The floor was warm, heated *Ondol*-style, where pipes from the kitchen's oven heat the bedroom floor, slightly elevated. Bedding was rolled on one side of the main room. A mother had laid her baby , perhaps 6 months old, on a blanket on the warm floor. She answered our team's questions directly. When did she last eat animal protein? One egg, two weeks ago. How many meals did she eat per day? Sometimes two meals per day, sometimes not. How did she prepare her meals? She sometimes added water to the food she prepared, to increase volume[11]. Had she gotten UNICEF or WFP feeding supplements? She wasn't sure what those were. We were three men asking, and no one thought to ask about breastfeeding. Dumb, lost opportunity that shows why teams need to be multi-gendered. Her answers felt genuine, but of course she was not alone. Our interpreter and an official from the Ministry of Agriculture accompanied us, their red badges working like a signal to be careful.

I stepped out of her house, turned the corner and found myself face-to-face with two children carrying water on their shoulders. The yoke carrying the vats was made of wood, the buckets aluminium. They

Figure 7.2 Children carrying water from a well, Nampo, South Pyongan Province. Courtesy of Eric Lafforgue.

looked strong, busy, dirty, worried, and in a hurry. They did not respond to my smile.

* * *

Back in the car, our conversation resumed. The young mother and her baby were on my mind.

'All the protein she ate was one egg, two weeks ago? Even on the farm, people don't get enough to eat?' I asked Tripathy.

Tripathy answered, 'Soya or bean paste is the main source of protein here. Officially, the daily energy requirement per North Korean person is 2,500 calories per day, consistent with international nutritional standards – the amount of energy a person needs to consume each day to maintain their current work level and body weight.' I kept quiet: the average American consumed more than 3,600 calories per day.

'In fact, North Koreans do not even consume half of the 2500-calorie requirement,' Tripathy answered. 'The rations have diminished drastically for the 16 million or so North Koreans who depend on them. Even the measly 375 grammes of cereal currently allocated are being reduced further. Slogans are springing up everywhere about the need to use less food.'

I mentioned that my UNICEF colleagues had indicated that over time, malnutrition modified the population's genetic make-up and I concluded, a little mystified, with a question, 'If the two Koreas were to become one again, the Southern half would be taller, healthier, and basically, smarter?'

Tripathy nodded, and said that one of the challenges of reunification would be to integrate a population that had been starved, physically and intellectually.

I looked through my window as we sped on the empty road, back to Pyongyang. Groups of people stood or sat in the fields we were passing. They were collecting last bits of harvest from the ground. It looked like wheat, or barley. The farmers looked up at our car. Men's faces were those of farmers, baked by the sun. Others appeared more 'urban'. I had heard that city folks were summoned to the countryside at harvest time. Perhaps I was projecting my own opinion onto them, but I would say that they seemed to dread the assignment. Further down, two women slammed the stalks with a wooden mortar, separating grains from the husk. Others had placed the ears of wheat on the road itself so that our tires would do the job by rolling over the stalks.

The scene reminded me of Japanese classic films portraying the whole village outside, during planting and harvest times. Villagers sang songs as they moved in rows. Were they hoping for an abundant harvest? Were they singing in unison? I really could not say, separated from them by more than just a car window.

* * *

The Crop and Food Assessment mission members presented their conclusions before departing the country. For the season spanning the end of 2010 to the first half of 2011, the mission report estimated that the DPRK would produce approximately 4.4 million tonnes of cereals from cooperative farms, individual plots on sloping land and household gardens. The national need for cereal was estimated at a little over five million tonnes of cereal equivalent.[12]

The reasons for this relatively poor harvest were mostly bad weather events, notably the longer winter and intense rainstorms in late August and early September. Late summer rains damaged the harvest which rotted on the ground because of poor transport and storage capacities. Localized flooding caused structural damage to irrigation canals and dams. These events were damaging enough to erase any gains from greater availability of fertilizer, pesticides, motorized farm equipment that actually worked, diesel and electricity.

In the long term, the team members explained, North Korea had to improve its potato storage and grain drying facilities to reduce losses and improve food safety; increase production of protein-rich commodities such as soybeans and beans, lentils, peas or peanuts and fish; and support private plots on sloping land and household gardens for households' food security.

The fourth and last strategy to strengthen food security was to bring in food from the outside. The DPRK intended to import about 300,000 tonnes of cereals from China. As to the rest of the deficit – 300,000 tonnes – the UN would make an appeal for food assistance on behalf of the DPRK. This assistance was destined for the most vulnerable groups such as children, pregnant and lactating women, the elderly and people in mountainous regions.

The food assessment mission knew that fundamentally North Korean agriculture desperately needed to produce more and better crops to feed more people. They recommended introducing a more diverse crop rotation with legumes, potatoes and pulse which would also help improve the protein content of the national diet. They also recommended more sustainable practices for soil regeneration.

Figure 7.3 Kitchen garden, Kaesong City. Photo by Carolyn Sauvage-Mar.

These proposed changes comported enormous implications. Such shifts would challenge both the technical knowledge and the types and amount of investment required.

To be sure, our recommendations remained within the existing political and economic system and did not discuss whether to liberalize North Korea's agriculture – and how. The mission noted why the Government would not entertain this line of discussion.

* * *

In the DPRK, aside from planning their daily communal chores, most North Koreans wake up in the morning with one worry: what will they and their family eat today? The North Korean regime exercised political control through food. It manipulated the availability, distribution, and price of it, often using tactics like rationing, targeted food distribution programmes, and controlling agricultural production. By creating dependence on the state for sustenance and limiting dissent by using hunger as a tool of control, it created situations where food insecurity was high, rewarding loyalty and punishing opposition through access to food.

One of Carolyn's worst memories is an image that evokes the link between food and extreme hardship. We were driving towards the China border on one of the coldest days of the year. Temperatures hovered around minus 15 Celsius (5 degrees F). Each village we passed was surrounded by fields, and groups of people were out making small piles of night soil or manure, and then posing colourful banners on or near them to commemorate their collective accomplishment, such as it was. The brutality of the cold was matched only by the cruelty of the demand on the people to be outside and the stupidity of the task. Once the date had been set, we assumed, the authorities were unflinching in imposing this mobilization campaign on the villagers even when temperatures made it dangerous. The tiny piles of fertilizer wouldn't cover one row of crops let alone an entire piece of land, and the people out there doing this make-work activity had to know this. Fertilizer was precious and making small piles of available night soil was not going to make the difference in next year's production nor cover up the shortage, whatever the exhortations. It was a cynical use of people's labour and one she found inexcusable.

Was our food aid prolonging the oppression? Not necessarily. To begin with, whilst the aid was limited in amount, the programme was focused and had a positive impact on the disadvantaged population it sought to help. The UN humanitarian programmes worked jointly through an integrated approach that addressed immediate needs in nutrition and agriculture, health, water and sanitation. These interventions were designed to combat stunting that occurs during pregnancy and the first two years of life. The management of severe acute malnutrition (SAM) continued to inform who and where to target assistance. To reduce the food gap in North Korea, WFP, UNICEF and other NGOs consistently addressed the nutrition needs and deficiencies among vulnerable children and pregnant and breastfeeding mothers. The operation also included a structured approach towards prevention and treatment of acutely malnourished children and women.

The FAO aimed to improve food and nutrition security through agricultural productivity, sustainable food production systems and innovative appropriate technologies such as enhancing production of soybean, vegetables, livestock and fish products. They worked mostly in the 90 counties in the southern part of the country where most of the food production took place. The UNDP funded rural development projects in seeds diversification, post-harvest losses, renewable rural energy and community-level disaster preparedness.

But I already knew that North Korea's structural problems in agriculture would remain. The Ministry of Agriculture remained hell bent on cereal production, continuing against evidence to push non-sustainable double cropping of wheat and barley after rice and maize. The soils were exhausted. With a very low level of mechanization and input, cereal production would not grow.

I also knew from past years that the international community would not come close to meeting the financial demands from this appeal. There would remain a gap. '*For this gap*,' I thought to myself, '*there is hunger*.' *And it's hard to push for change when you are hungry*.'

Chapter 8

ASHES OVER YEONPYEONG

Relationship breakthrough with Government over UNDP projects – Coal mine – North Korea bombs Yeonpyeong Island – A colleague is 'citizen-arrested' – Christmas and New Year among the international community – The UNDP team – Family tourism: Mount Kumgang, Kaesong, DMZ – Musings about this past year

On the road to Wonsan, huge concrete pillars frame the tunnels' entrance, like giant sentinels. These pillars can be dynamited to block army tanks invading from the East Sea. Beyond the East Sea looms Japan, Korea's nineteenth-century colonizers. In 1950, the Americans landed on these shores. In North Korea, the past is never past.

* * *

The end of our first full year in North Korea was approaching and I felt more confident to address certain aspects of my relationship with the Government. Our disagreement over the pace of project development still made things tense. My team and Headquarters were writing UNDP projects and getting them approved as fast as possible, but never fast enough. I understood that my counterparts in Government felt their own pressure to deliver results. And yes, at the working level, they were trying to make things work, even Mr Song, in his own distinctively antagonistic ways! Their cross to bear included having to interpret and operationalize our requests through more recalcitrant parts of the regime, such as the Party or the Security system. Sometimes they obtained a green light and sometimes they came back to us, openly frustrated, because the solution which we had thought up together was simply not going to work. I soon learned to more carefully listen to what they would tell me, in half-disguised sentences, about their constraints. In fact, they passed on plenty of information about the black box that was the North Korean regime. In return, I realized, I could use them to pass my messages upwards. So I invited Choe and Song to the office.

Our conversation started with some difficulty. I recalled the context of suspicion that floated over UNDP among donors – not just the USA – at the time when the office closed, then re-opened just a few months back. We had to be extra careful, I concluded.

'The suspension of the office was totally unjustified!' Song answered.

'Perhaps it was, but we at UNDP showed a strong commitment to re-open as soon as possible. The reason for it is the value we attach to our past years of cooperation.'

Song objected that the past years did not justify delays in re-starting projects.

'Mr. Song,' I answered, 'the projects take this long because donors' hesitancy is high and frankly went even higher after the Cheonan incident.' I then asked for a measure of trust in each other and for more leeway in the choice of projects (more locally-oriented, less capacity-building), and time. I had rehearsed this little speech in my head all morning, unsure how far I could go. I wasn't sure if I was overstepping or finally doing what needed to be done. But I pressed on.

The next meeting, Choe visited the office alone. He sat down and without introduction, he began, 'We decided that you, Jerome, are not the obstacle.' He did not bother to elaborate. *Poof! Just like that?* This simple sentence felt surreal. I was taken aback with this swift reversal in the Government's attitude. After months of frustration and tiptoeing through bureaucratic fog, could my little plea for trust, a few days, earlier really have changed their entire approach?

Trust. The word is so loaded with misconceptions when it comes to the DPRK. To be sure, I have come across several aid programmes that were suspended because a donor agency pointed out that the North Korean side had not delivered on its side of the agreement. I also came across situations when invoking trust or the tired old concept of 'win-win' just did not fly. The North Korean side, in that situation, seemed to prefer that all parties end up being worse off if they could not outright win the deal. The 'win-win' compromise I offered somehow ended up looking, to their eyes, like their loss.

One reason for the Government's sudden cooperativeness, I came to realize, was that the months spent in the country with people like Song, Choe, and others had created a bond of trust that was not easily discarded.

The people we spoke to inside the North Korean Government knew of our challenges and difficulties. They knew that running programmes in North Korea was not an easy sell abroad. They may not have supported the sinking of that South Korean navy vessel. Once you had them believe that you did your best and you were – for now – their best ally, there was a chance that they'd advocate with the higher spheres of the regime to keep working with you. It is a delicate balance. In truth, people outside the DPRK sometimes looked at me with suspicion, as if I had gone soft. A few even hinted I was suffering from Stockholm Syndrome – sympathizing with my captors, absorbing their logic. But I saw it differently. My job was to build bridges where others saw walls. It wasn't about sympathy – it was about staying human in a system designed to dehumanize both sides, and to find enough common ground to support the UN's work to improve the lives of the North Korean people.

It was important to remain mindful of the particular context in which we worked. In order to effectively collaborate with the North Korean Government, I had to constantly shift my attitude between sympathetic understanding and sceptical judgment. I learned to hear their rationalizations without expressing agreement. I could integrate their point of view whilst maintaining my own. Such tightrope walking, though wearing, became a second nature over time.

The Government did not completely give up and tried to get UNDP Headquarters to fire our New York-based backstopping Officer. I assured Choe and Song that the gentleman had nothing to do with our difficulties, but no matter. I strongly advised them to let the matter go. Incredibly, we were soon informed that another colleague was taking over the portfolio! I never knew what transpired in New York.

As we neared the end of our first year in the DPRK, I felt a sense of accomplishment. We had overcome various obstacles and survived winter. I felt my relationship with the Government could improve from here on. Our daily lives had become more routine and our apartment more liveable. UNDP could continue to launch new projects on solid operational and control foundations.

Or so it seemed. I was about to learn an important lesson: when things start to improve and feel normal in North Korea, you should prepare for anything.

* * *

To accelerate the approval process for our rural renewable energy projects, I visited the Yaksu Cooperative Farm which was interested in renewable energy, and a coal mine in Kangso county, in South Pyongan Province, south-west of the capital city,. The person accompanying us on the visit was Mrs O Young Kim from the Ministry of Electric Power Industry. Mrs O always dressed in a simple, business-like get-up. Her hair was permed as was nearly mandatory with middle-aged, presumably married women. She knew her stuff, and she was very interested in getting energy to rural areas.

I had begun to notice that my government counterparts tended to come in two contrasting personality styles. I would quietly called each distinct type 'the adept and the inept' or 'the efficient and the officiant'. More seriously, these parodies represented to me the two ends of a spectrum made of a professional expert at one end and a political operator at the other end. I had placed my antagonist Mr Song in the latter category. I felt that the professionals knew their business, while the political operators focused more on orthodoxy. So far, the sycophants were always men, while qualified professionals included women. Fortunately, the Government usually recognized competency and allowed the professionals to represent them in our project negotiations. Mrs O was definitely a professional.

Kangso County had abundant coal reserves mainly anthracite and lignite for generating electricity, but of low quality. Coal extraction, processing, and combustion were inefficient and polluting, with significant energy losses over poor transmission lines. We visited the farm and Kangso coal mine to explore clean technologies for heating in rural homes, service institutions, and agricultural processing.

Figure 8.1 Entrance to a coal mine in Kangso County. Photo by Jerome Sauvage.

Our office had recruited an energy specialist. Zharas Takenov hailed from a Central Asian country rich in oil. He was a renewable energy specialist and accomplished modern painter in his spare time, but as a younger man, to finance his studies, he'd been a professional boxer, a national sport in his country. He knew all about renewable energy. Growing up under Soviet rule, he understood his mission in the DPRK from a personal perspective. 'You see,' he'd begin, voice measured,

> out here in the countryside, it's different. Pyongyang is its own world – lit up, controlled, a stage set for those who need to believe in the performance. But out here? Darkness. Not metaphorical, real. Night falls, and the world disappears. No hum of refrigerators, no streetlamps, no flicker of televisions behind thin curtains. Just the wind, the cold, the dark. I know this silence. I grew up in it, back in the Soviet days, when Moscow had the power, and we – the so-called 'resource hub' – had whatever they allowed us.

He would lean forward, his knuckles tapping the car window, slow, deliberate:

> Renewable energy – it's not just about power. It's about independence. Give a village a solar panel, a wind turbine, a battery system, and suddenly, they don't have to wait. They don't have to depend. They don't have to beg the state to notice them. It's small, but small things matter. I learned that in the ring – one opening, one inch, can change everything. The Party sees energy as control and yes, I see it as freedom.

He'd smile, but there was weight behind it. 'Of course, they won't say no to our suggestions. But I know, just like in the Soviet days, that change doesn't come in a revolution overnight. It comes in moments. A single house lit up when the rest of the valley is dark. A farmer who works an extra hour because he has light. A child who reads at night and grows up asking questions.' His fingers twitched slightly, as if itching for a brush, a canvas. 'I used to think my power was in my fists. Now? It's in this. In kilowatts and battery packs, in wind and sun. In the idea that maybe, just maybe, the people out here won't have to wait for Pyongyang's permission to step out of the dark.'

We approached the mine where a slag heap perhaps 30 metres high dominated the whole town. By the pit though, everything was quiet. The mine was simply not active. A few men walked idly around, looking curiously at us. The mine management greeted us without formality, and I indicated I would like, out of pure curiosity, to see the pit. Mrs O and I were given plastic helmets, but no one else got one. I resolutely walked down along rusty tracks going straight down a pit, followed by a hesitant Mrs O and my national programme officer. After perhaps 30 metres down, my international colleagues begged me to return, explaining that nothing in this mineshaft seemed safe. I reluctantly returned. Had I pushed further, would I have uncovered something they didn't want me to see? Or was I simply witnessing in plain view a primitive, unsafe and unproductive mine?

During the meeting, I informed the management of Kangso mine that without electricity, which is necessary for lighting, operating jackhammers, and extracting coal, funding coal extraction equipment would be ineffective. I suggested procuring pumps to remove water from submerged seams if electricity was available to operate them. The relationship between Ministry staff and mine management appeared strained. The Ministry prohibited photos of the mine, while the mine manager and technicians were not opposed to it. The tension between the Ministry and mine officials seemed pronounced, with both sides maintaining their positions. The Yaksu Cooperative Farm personnel was straightforward to work with. They expressed an interest in using all forms of renewable energy. While the Kangso mine supplied them with coal, the community sought to improve energy use by utilizing smaller coal brickettes that enhanced coal combustion with modified stoves. They presented various improved coal stoves and provided figures from tests evaluating thermal performance.

The other possible renewable energy technology application consisted of a rice husk gasification power plant that could be installed on the farm. Rice husk generated from the existing rice mill could produce around 100 kilowatts of electricity. The ash generated from gasifier would be utilized or sold as valuable fertilizer.[1]

We pushed for a phased approach, knowing that without careful groundwork, our efforts could be easily derailed. We would need to be careful to document that the extracted coal was exclusively destined for local utilization. They agreed, though I sensed their impatience to get started. We worked to turn the information into a project document to be submitted for funding.

* * *

November was here. Exactly one year in North Korea. The Christmas and New Year holiday was approaching, and with it, a bittersweet contrasting sense of warmth and isolation. For the international community, this was a rare occasion for festivity, a reminder of life beyond the sealed world we inhabited. The Swedish Embassy ushered in the season with the St. Lucia's Day, a tradition where candlelight pierced the darkness. Nowhere had I ever felt so keenly the significance of that contrast. Nighttime can be so dark in North Korea. The embassies from Europe and beyond did their part, offering small but treasured luxuries: sweets, spiced wines, cakes – oh, how we craved cakes. Very few internationals had access to an oven (we did), and anything freshly-baked carried with it the warmth of home. We hosted as often as we could, too, trying to create friendliness where there might be little.

And then there was the RAC! Our club, our refuge. The RAC opened most week-ends and sometimes during the week. Koreans did not ever step inside, at least not when expatriates were there. I heard that during the heydays of the mid-1990s, when many more NGOs and UN personnel traipsed through North Korea, the RAC was open every day. The RAC still kept that out-of-this-world feel. It was located inside the former East German Embassy. The architecture was disconcerting – walls slashed at unnatural angles, neither square nor round, as if designed to keep people unsteady. It was impossible to feel at ease, let alone welcome. Hidden off to the side was a door. Small, unassuming, oddly placed – like an afterthought, or an escape hatch into another world. In a way, that's exactly what it was. A thick curtain concealed the RAC's entrance, and stepping inside felt like crossing a threshold into something secret, something unreal. The room was cavernous, but not in a way that made it grand – more like an old theatre long past its prime. The ceiling stretched high above us, and dim lamps cast just enough light to make out worn-out couches slumped in a corner. The long bar at the far end was lined with bottles, arranged with care. Russians and Mongolians brought their own vodka; British and Irish their respective whiskey and gin; the French brought Cognac and Cointreau; and there was always soju and sake. Young volunteers dusted glasses, their movements slow, methodical. It was dark in a way that made the space both vast and intimate, a contradiction that fit the entire experience of being here.

A stranger greeted me as I entered.

'Welcome to the RAC. The name stands for Random Access Club . . .'

I must have looked confused. He hesitated, then added,

'You know . . . random access to monitor projects.'

I didn't laugh, although I should have. What a perfect metaphor for the strange limbo we all lived in – half-monitors, half-intruders, granted just enough access to move through this world without ever truly belonging to it. We were sometimes ten and sometimes fifty.

In the RAC, we could finally meet other expatriates whom we otherwise didn't often see, as well as international visitors who stayed in hotels, were in the know and were granted permission to visit the diplomatic area. Ambassadors socialized with university teachers from Canada, Russians and Europeans and businessmen-cum-humanitarians from New Zealand; Egyptian Telecomm employees danced with Polish shipping agents; Russia's Tass News Services discussed with Western journalists; and of course sometimes tourists, who dynamic tour operators brought on visits to North Korea, came and gawked at us. By necessity, the humanitarian crowd is good at making – and losing – friends quickly. They'll meet on some other theatre of operations in another part of the world and know to let their guards down and relax for a fleeting moment.

We watched the 2010 Football World Cup inside the RAC, including the DPRK's terrible defeat to Portugal. For some unexplainable reason, the match had been shown live in Pyongyang. We came rooting for the North Koreans, hopeful, reminding ourselves of North Korea's achievement in England in 1966, when DPRK became the first Asian country to qualify past the first round. Sadly, this time was not to be. We all booed Ronaldo after he acrobatically and gratuitously scored his team's 7th goal. Did he have to hammer another nail, humiliate the opposite team, and act like he was having fun doing so? The waitresses at the Friendship Club cried unconsolably that day.

Once only, towards the end of our mission, things went a little out of control at the RAC. Three humanitarian NGO workers were commemorating their permanent departure from the DPRK. A few days earlier, they had hung a red banner from a window down one of the buildings in Munsudong with the golden letters '*Get Hot!*' in the purest communist style. That evening, everyone was milling around inside the RAC when a cry was heard above the music and the conversations. 'Here they come!' Soon, the first bars of *I Gotta Feeling*, courtesy the Black Eyed Peas, and a current hit at the RAC, came on, repetitive, insistent. *'Tonight's gonna be a good night!'* All heads turned towards the entrance door. A group marched in. They had donned yellow and red plastic construction helmets, undershirts and fake tattoos showing the North Korean flag and the hammer and sickle. They danced their way up to the bar to clapping and cheers. At the end of the evening, the three guests of honour stood atop the bar to the sound of '*I'm Leaving on a Jet Plane*,' sung by Peter, Paul and Mary, and one by one jumped into a row of hands and arms webbed in a long mat to collect them onto the safety of their embrace. Somehow word of the party reached the North Korean authorities who didn't look kindly on joking around with the flag, especially in public. Since a UN colleague was indirectly involved, I was convoked at the MFA and had to make amends on their behalf. There were orders for non-UN staff expulsion and various reprimands. Also, WFP decided to not host the RAC for a while. A friend's concert took place inside our place (without flags) but everyone sorely missed the originality and the warmth of the RAC. I hoped it re-opened after our departure.

We were beginning to carve out a kind of home, however transitory. Our apartment was now presentable and we enjoyed welcoming everyone. We were settling in, though I wasn't sure whether that was comfort or a refuge from the strange environment.

* * *

Following my breakthrough conversation with Choe and Song a few weeks earlier, I had begun to hope that, despite the difficulties, we might bend the system to deliver our projects and aid to those most in need. Then came the bombardment – and with it, a reminder of the limits of good intentions in a state built for brinkmanship.

Early that morning, I checked the internet and read the headlines:

> *Following a South Korean artillery exercise in southern waters, the North fired around 170 artillery shells and rockets at a South Korean island named Yeonpyeong, hitting both military and civilian targets.*

The exchange of fire lasted just over an hour. South Korean F-15s and F-16s scrambled to the area but did not engage North Korean targets – perhaps because the North didn't initiate a third barrage. This wasn't just another provocation; it was the first full-scale artillery battle between the two Koreas since the 1970s, and one of the most serious attacks on the South since the 1953 Armistice. The Western media quickly framed it as a disproportionate response to a South Korean military exercise in disputed waters. From where I stood, it wasn't so simple. Who fired first? Did the South knowingly provoke the North? Or was this an overreaction, a show of force meant to send a message? Standing in Pyongyang, I was acutely aware that my perspective was different from the analysts and commentators watching from afar. I now had a front-row seat to how quickly things could escalate on the Korean Peninsula.

By lunchtime, the tension in the air was inescapable. I was quite surprised to see a group of Korean staffers from UN offices – including from our own UNDP office marching out of the Munsudong diplomatic compound, carrying wooden rifles. Going to a rally, no doubt. Rumours spread: airspace interdictions, suspended commercial flights. Some embassies quietly discussed whether to evacuate until the rhetoric cooled. The veteran expatriates were unshaken. '*These things will blow over*,' they assured me. Maybe. But I wasn't willing to bet on blind confidence. I visualized the Korean peninsula from above – a satellite's-eye view, feeling like a tiny dot in this ominous landscape. Our security arrangements had to be evaluated immediately. I pulled up the UN security plan. Our responsibility was clear: international personnel and North Korean contractors fell under UN jurisdiction and the Government had an obligation to support the UN for it. There were at all time about fifty internationally recruited UN staff and twenty-five family members.

Regarding our contracted national staff, UNDP employed 15 North Korean staff and 33 family members. Our obligations would have us include them in any evacuation. Whereas the authorities would certainly not permit it, I knew I'd have to formally ask, if it came to that. Meanwhile, I skimmed the year's incident log, all concerning international personnel so far: five medical evacuations, including a broken arm, a motorcycle accident, nothing like *this*.

I read with a certain sense of irony the latest quarterly security report prepared by our specialists:

> *Potential for military conflict: Low. Impact of military conflict: High. Whereas political tension between the DPRK and the USA, Japan, and Republic of Korea is rising due to the recent missile launch and renewed UN sanctions, the DPRK Government has shown signs of re-engagement in bilateral and six-party talks.*

That assessment had aged poorly. Here, as in many other parts of the world, certainty was an illusion. With the UN Security Team, we updated our evacuation plan: exact list of personnel still in-country; suspension of all travel outside the capital; designated rally points; assigned vehicles for emergency movement. We sent a car to check the road to Sinuiju, the town with Dandong, China, across the border. We relayed all updates to the Korean authorities, who responded with their usual impassivity. We coordinated with NGOs and European Embassies and agreed as per international agreements to share responsibility for international NGOs in case of evacuation.

* * *

Tensions had affected everyone in town, seeping into the daily rhythms of life. A few days later, I received troubling news – one of our experts had been arrested and released within a few hours. He was a quiet northern European man, fond of wandering the authorized parts of the City with his camera, capturing excellent scenes of Pyongyang's daily life. I was not involved in his release – the office's senior national staff responsible for liaison with the Government had been called to the police station and had him released. I felt very unhappy with the incident and lodged a complaint with the MFA. The expert recounted the incident to me. He had been taking photographs of a statue, something he had done many times before, unaware of two women sitting on the floor against a nearby wall. One of them, a short middle-aged woman suddenly charged toward him, her arms flailing, her face twisted in anger. She grabbed his camera. Startled, he resisted – only to find she was stronger than he expected. The struggle escalated until she finally wrenched it from his grip. Within seconds, a dozen onlookers surrounded him, their collective hostility unmistakable. A policeman arrived, silenced the crowd with a curt gesture, and motioned for the lady and our colleague to follow. The crowd went along, swelling in numbers, murmuring. He was taken to a police station – a nondescript building without signs or markings. There, the policeman made a phone call, then pointed to a bench. Our colleague sat, waiting. Thinking. Then he knew. 'The ice boxes!' he told me later, shaking his head. 'They were in plain sight under the mural. Those women were selling food. Street vending is tolerated but not legal. My photos might have exposed them, and they panicked. They thought they'd be punished.' Shortly after, an officer from the MFA arrived, took the camera, and, along with the policeman, carefully reviewed the images. They deleted the offending ones, then returned the camera without further explanation.

At my meeting with MFA Head of the International Department Mr Yun Tae Song to discuss the case, I asked, keeping my voice neutral, 'What exactly was the problem with the pictures?'

'Our country must protect our security, as you know,' he replied in a careful tone.

I inquired further to determine if there was a law prohibiting photography. Mr Yun responded with some frustration and discomfort but did not specify a law. It appeared that taking photographs was not allowed unless specifically authorized. This interpretation differed from the typical understanding that actions are generally permitted unless explicitly forbidden by law. Then Mr Yun's next comment took me by surprise.

'We all need to be careful,' he said slowly. 'These are difficult times.'

There was a quiet heaviness in his voice that I had never heard before. Something like a plea for unspoken understanding. He wasn't just talking about the rules; he was reminding me of something hidden. *We all need to be careful, understand?*

That evening, as dusk fell over Pyongyang, my perception of the city had somehow altered. I had peeled back a layer, having seen how an authoritarian system had transformed the street vendor, whom I generally perceived as a potential casualty of the regime, to an active enforcer of that system. Despite feeling more comfortable in the DPRK, one artillery exchange reminded us that we were still outsiders, used by the regime to reinforce fear of the outside world.

* * *

Thankfully, that past year, our daughter and her then-boyfriend (he is now her husband) had provided a much-needed distraction during their visit. Together, we journeyed south to Mount Kumgang, Kaesong and the Demilitarized Zone. Among the three revered mountains of

Figure 8.2 On Mount Kumgang. Photo by Jerome Sauvage.

Figure 8.3 The Demilitarized Zone viewed from the North. Photo by Jerome Sauvage.

North Korea, Kumgang stood out as the most enchanting. No surprise UNESCO recently added it to its World Heritage list. The persistent fog from the nearby sea lent an ethereal quality to the trees; steep stairs ascended like ladders; waterfalls streamed through unique rock formations and carvings. Many hillside carvings and statues were linked to Buddhism, underscoring the mountain's historical importance to Korean Buddhist tradition. More recent carvings bore quotes from Kim Il Sung, merging political messages with the scenic allure.

From Mount Kumgang, we made our way to Kaesong, the UNESCO World Heritage Site showcasing the history and culture of the Koryo Dynasty from the tenth to fourteenth centuries. The old City was like no other place in the DPRK. History was everywhere, vividly maintained and represented. The town's layout, according to geomantic principles, its architecture, palaces, institutions and the tomb complex, reflected the integration of Buddhism, Confucianism, and Taoism. According to the UNESCO pamphlet, Kaesong represented 'the assimilation of the cultural spiritual and political values of the states that existed prior to Korea's unification under the Koryo Dynasty'. I could feel the weight of history in words such as 'unified Koryo civilization'. I even felt that the people we interacted with – notably our guide, an elegant and knowledgeable woman – were different from people in other parts of the country. Perhaps this was due to their exposure to South Koreans and others, who had visited Kaesong in the thousands. Reassuringly, the DPRK was not prepared to erase the heart of ancient Korea, in all its historical cultural glory and sophistication.

UNESCO had done a great job and the government had complied to make sure that Kaesong would remain a World Heritage Site. They kept the heights of newer buildings lower than the historic sites; the original alignment of ancient roads was preserved; the visual harmony in form and colour of buildings was controlled and the surrounding natural landscape was preserved to show 'the relationship of *feng shui* [the ancient Asian practice that focuses on aligning the environment with life and well-being] with individual historical sites'.

The touristic part of the town, equipped to receive what I imagined had been busloads of visitors from South Korea in more peaceful times, was essentially empty. We were the only tourists. We ate a delicious meal with many of the *banchan* (side dishes) not found in Pyongyang unless on special occasions.

* * *

Our tour ended at the DMZ. This heavily fortified border separating North and South Korea symbolizes the enduring state of technical conflict, with no peace treaty signed, despite the 1953 armistice. Various efforts to reduce violence and increase cooperation, including the removal of guard posts and mines, didn't prevent the fact that the DMZ continues to be a place of high tension, and the situation remains volatile with the potential for escalation at any time.

The DMZ seen from North Korea was not as striking as when I had approached it from the southern side, where you could drive up hills and survey vast amounts of territories and understand the vastness of this 200-kilometres long, deadly zone. Here in the DPRK, our access was limited to one entry point centred on the long, low buildings standing over the demarcation line. In these buildings, a cease fire was agreed. Should peace happen, it would be discussed right there.

I approached the whole site wearily, thinking of my job representing the UN in North Korea. The UN had been the North's formal enemy in the 1950-1953 war. I knew that today, the UN Command Military Armistice Commission (UNMAC) was not representing the whole UN any more: it is a US-led command composed of representatives from various countries, including South Korea, the United Kingdom, and other nations that have pledged to respond jointly to any threats to South Korean security.

Still, seeing the UN flag hoisted on the South's side of the DMZ, where American and South Korean soldiers stood guard against the North, was a little disconcerting. I heard how in the mid-1990s the first sight of the UN flags and vehicles unnerved the North Koreans too, as the UN humanitarians began programmes. The population needed to be educated about the UN's new, friendlier posture.

Old role, new role, same role? Were thirty years of UN cooperation enough to erase the misgivings of the war? Were the devastating sanctions imposed upon the people of the DPRK not, in their eyes, the expression of continued Western enmity clothed in legal international Security Council resolutions? As the UN Coordinator, I had been careful to render accounts of my work to all my 'patrons' in Pyongyang and most notably the three members of the UN Security Council present in North Korea: China, Russia and the United Kingdom. Yet these efforts did not attenuate my Western affiliations, nor the fact that the UN was based in New York City and that most of our programme financing came from OECD donors. There was nothing that I could do about these facts. But one thing that I resolved to do better was to make North Korea's real situation better known abroad, in all its complexities and in all its suffering.

The *Cheonan* incident and the Yeonpyeong bombardment had shown me how fragile the armistice was, sixty years after it was signed, but at the same time that we had to find a way to keep our work going.

The UN operational agencies could not address the absence of a lasting peace agreement on the Korean Peninsula. But there were issues and problems that loomed large beyond this single conflict and required global solutions, like climate change or the movement of goods or people across borders. Just like most other countries, North Korea was also keen to protect its natural resources and participate in this global world. The UN 'just' had to find a way to bring the DPRK to the global table.

And beyond everyday frustrations, we had to treasure moments of levity. On our visit, for example, Carolyn, from her viewpoint above the DMZ, spotted a US Army officer walking briskly on his side of the border. She spontaneously called and waved to him. There was something so relaxed and so genuine to her shout out from the North that the officer looked up, which caused our guide to tense up. The American officer kept walking but this gave us all a good laugh. It was one of those times when you could allow yourself to dream that this absurd border and its millions of landmines and fortifications could be eliminated with laughter and good will.

Part II

Working within the System (2011)
Engagement and Compromise

Attempts, Optimism and Creative Diplomacy

Chapter 9

SETTLING IN

Strengthening the office's operations and programmes – Seeing project results in energy – Our home – Carolyn gets a car – A walk in Moran Park

The UN aid programme in North Korea was a paradox of size versus significance. It was one of the smallest UN programmes worldwide compared to other developing countries of similar population size and development level. And yet, in the absence of the usual multilateral 'biggies' – World Bank, Asian Development Bank, European Commission – the UN in North Korea became the largest multinational presence in North Korea.

* * *

As 2011 rolled in, things looked up for UNDP. We made progress on the finance, personnel and programme fronts. The office had reopened with a strong focus on financial controls, a major issue after the 2007 US Senate investigation. The North Korean government signed a Memorandum of Understanding that committed to strict conditions: (1) every expense had to be reviewed by international staff; (2) international staff had complete, daily access to our accounts at the FTB; and (3) all banking and reconciliation were to be handled exclusively by international staff.

Implementing this Memorandum was more complex than just writing it. North Korea essentially had no functioning banking sector. The state-controlled FTB was the only financial institution with any point of contact into the international system. Every international organization used it, including us. UNDP remained concerned about operational risks due to FTB practices over which we had no control, echoing problems that surfaced before 2007. We explored alternatives. Briefly, we had hopes for what the expat community called the 'Egyptian bank', run by Orascom, the Egyptian company behind the country's only official mobile phone network. While they circulated local currency, they couldn't offer proper banking services. It became clear that FTB was the only viable option. FTB was working closely with Chinese banks, and at the time still connected to international financial exchanges. Without it, we would not have an operational platform to import goods, pay local staff or contractors, or receive funds. We negotiated tighter protocols, ensuring only international staff could act as signatories on financial forms. Software was introduced to automate accounting and minimize the use of manual checks.

As regards personnel, our UNDP team had come together. All positions were filled: programme specialists, finance officers, energy and statistics experts. Our international colleagues came from around the world – India, Iraq, the Gambia, Eritrea, Mexico. One staff person brought along a young family. North Korea's isolation required people with strong internal balance, sustained by life's smallest pleasures: a walk outside, a good friend, a quiet evening or convivial gatherings in living rooms. Some staff became pillars of our community, engaging in soccer, tennis or yoga classes, organizing book clubs, film nights. A member of the fledgling French office in Pyongyang even organized an art exhibit immodestly titled '*Autumnales de Pyongyang*' – a nod to the season – during which we discovered the talent among our expatriate community. The relative isolation gave time for art, music, and friendships to bloom.

On a visit to the gym to work out, Carolyn encountered two local teenagers lounging on the weightlifting equipment. As she got on a treadmill, the girls chattered away, presumably gossiping about the things teenagers do. But then one of them dramatically brought her hand to her chest, lifted her head and belted out a perfect rendition of Celine Dion's iconic song from the movie *Titanic*, *My Heart Will Go On*, singing with fervour 'Near, Far, wherever you are . . .' Some things transcend borders without issue.

Among our national staff a range of types and talent also emerged. Most were in their thirties, a few older. There was "Mr. An", a former table tennis champion; Mrs Ba, brilliant and devoted; and gentle "Mr. Din", the office dreamer. "Mr. Choe", the Agriculture Officer had a penchant for recreational marijuana. Occasionally Carolyn would stop by the office and report that she smelled marijuana smoke. She thought this as inappropriate as funny. Cannabis, during office hours? This struck her as incongruous but struck a note of reassuring associations from her days of California hippie freedom. She also was unsure if anyone else was noticing since a large part of her women's network would probably have zero experience with the weed in question, but maybe some of the younger staff? After asking around, she discovered through Canadian teacher friends that when they taught English to middle and high schoolers, the students entered the classroom smelling of recently smoked marijuana. In a sobering tone, they surmised this may have helped to dull hunger as the school day was long and although food provision was mysterious to outsiders, meals were probably intermittent.

National staff received rare exposure to foreign ideas. This made them privileged but also suspect. They lived under constant scrutiny, tainted in the eyes of the State by their daily contact with us. How could they not be influenced by the concepts they heard – rights-based programming, transparency, and international standards that clashed with local doctrine?

Gabriel García Márquez famously said that everyone has three lives: a public life, a private life, and a secret life. In the DPRK, a friend of ours who had been working with the North Korean people since the mid-1990s once described a similar layering comprising of a public and a private side, but even deeper, more complex and even more secret. In *Nothing to Envy*, the then Beijing bureau chief of the *Los Angeles Times* Barbara Demick describes how North Koreans must maintain privacy and secrecy, even in their own lives. While not explicitly detailing how they specifically keep secrets from each other, she emphasizes the deeply controlled nature of North Korean society, where individuals are wary of revealing true feelings and beliefs.[1]

National staff working for international organizations were among the few civilians allowed to travel abroad. But even this was riddled with restrictions. For example, I witnessed how a seemingly simple project activity – sending a female nurse on a training to Southeast Asia – became a logistical nightmare for the reason that North Koreans couldn't travel abroad alone. The international officer at that Agency suggested that the male doctor accompany the nurse, but a man and woman traveling together was deemed not appropriate. The North Korean side insisted that the local administrators, who were all men, go and train the nurses upon their return. The Agency offered alternatives – pairing the head nurse with another woman, finding female project managers – which were flatly rejected.

I witnessed another example of cultural difference during an annual UNDP office retreat, designed to strengthen team spirit. The whole office travelled to Wonsan, stayed at the Tongmyong Hotel, and grilled fish and meat on the beach. Whenever I travelled with the team, the atmosphere of camaraderie was warm and genuine. North Koreans like to do things themselves: there was always someone who could build a fire, someone who cooked well, someone who sang beautifully. On the beach, we organized the usual team-building games, and I discovered that easy-going competitiveness matched with fair play did not reign supreme among my national colleagues. A simple hopping race on the sand, meant to encourage healthy team cooperation, quickly devolved into enthusiastic cheating. While some objected to the cheating, many genuinely could not see what was wrong with it.

That moment of conflicting perspectives turned out to be an apt prelude to the session I had planned with our newly appointed Ethics Officer, who happened to be in the region and joined us at the retreat. The UNDP Ethics Office itself was a recent creation – born of an external investigative panel's recommendations after the 2007 U.S. Senate inquiry – intended to guarantee that anyone, anywhere, could report misconduct without fear of reprisal. At the retreat, the officer explained ethics not as a rigid rulebook but as a living framework of subjective, adaptable, and learned values. In the rule-driven culture of the UNDP, this was already a quiet revolution: we were being asked to weigh decisions not by the letter of regulations, but by the spirit of our shared values. In North Korea, however, I found out that values were not an open subject for discussion – they were dictated, fixed, unquestionable. I suspected it would take time for this more fluid and self-reflective approach to take root.

* * *

UNDP projects showed results. I was especially pleased with our renewable rural energy programme. Zharas and I visited the counties which I had visited in South Pyongan province at the beginning of my stay. We entered the houses of two farmers where UNDP had installed wind turbines inside their homes. These were small wind turbines, 5 metres high with 300 watts of installed capacity charging individual 12 volts batteries. With it the farmer said he could operate such electric items as two bulbs, a TV, a DVD or a karaoke system with amplifier. When asked, the two farmers each explained that they had paid US$150 for the wind turbine, and spent $5.00 on annual maintenance cost. To charge a full battery took approximately 4 hours and could last about 7 days, depending upon the wind speed and the state of the battery. In the village, neighbours could each bring their battery to get it charged at the farmers' houses. When asked what they liked best with this admittedly small improvement, both replied: 'to have electricity when I want it'. In this county alone, over 100 turbines were installed in people's households and in farm offices. They were entirely locally made in the Daily

Necessities Factory in the adjacent county of Sukchon. Batteries were made locally or in China.

We went to Pyongsong city to see a larger mast (10 Kilo Watts) and a solar panel we had delivered at the County Hospital. For the whole cost of $30,000[2] , we installed a 5kW wind turbine made in China and a solar panel, backing up the work of two operation rooms and two emergency rooms with which the hospital conducted operations and emergency obstetric during ever-frequent electricity cuts. $30,000 to demonstrate to the North Koreans how to save lives and so mothers don't die during labour.

After I left North Korea, Zharas told me that the hydro turbines had been successfull installed in Hoechang county – the first site I visited with Mr Han, the County manager. The new infrastructure would provide enough electricity for local farms and their food factories to support the people of Hoechang.

The project eventually operated on 4 sites, with 2 sites in South Pyongan Province, 1 site in South Hwanghae Province and 1 in Kangwon Province. The renewable energy projects which UNDP implemented included the 600 kW Small Hydro Power rehabilitation; hundreds of solar hot water systems, pumping system; biogas pig farm systems; energy efficient stoves working with biomass and with coal; energy efficient buildings; solar systems and household biogas systems. The project also introduced wind turbine technology and soon, the people knew how to build their own wind blades and equip their own home turbines.

These simple systems were built 'in hard', therefore not easy to divert. We could visit them and monitor their use. They directly helped people, who quickly learned how to improve them.

* * *

In parallel to the projects, our personal lives settled into a rhythm. To be sure, the trifecta of modern convenience – water, heat, and electricity – rarely visited all at once. One was the norm, three a miracle. It became a running joke: 'Quick, take a shower – there's warm water!' But we adapted. Our electric hand mixer routinely failed against cake batter, but our gas oven triumphed. It allowed Carolyn to bake chocolate chip cookies and deliver them to the UNDP team on June 25th – North Korea's Day of Anti-US Struggle – with a note: 'In Friendship'.

We explored restaurants where locals dined too: a burger joint vaguely echoing McDonald's, a pizzeria founded and supplied by an Italian communist, a bar serving dried Alaska pollock or *Hwangtae*,

Figure 9.1 Pyongsong Hospital Windmill. Courtesy of Zharas Takenov.

Figure 9.2 Villager with blade for her house's wind turbine, Samsan Cooperative Farm, South Hwanghae. Courtesy of Zharas Takenov.

Figure 9.3 Vitamin A distribution. Photo by Jerome Sauvage.

which was dried by freezing/drying in the cold winter months, which produces a more intense flavour and dark yellow colour. We sat at the bar's counter where patrons would slap whole fish on the counter to break it into pieces to eat with ample mugs of beer. We ate dried fish with our fingers. Unfortunately, we stopped when a medical doctor friend told us that dried pollock could contain parasitic worms, that could be a concern if the fish was not properly cooked or frozen. Best of all were what we considered the world's best cold noodles – *naengmyeon* served all day at the Koryo Hotel and which we paid with local currency[3].

Home life and office logistics often blurred. Early on, internet access became urgent. My deputy and our IT staff had early on set up a direct Wi-Fi link to the WFP office 300 metres away. With that, we connected to the world. I spoke to my daughter and to my son on Skype, trying to sound casual: 'Hey, how's everything going?' But inside, I was flooded with relief. We weren't entirely cut off. We used DVDs and watched *The Wire*, followed Obama's re-election via the satellite radio, and at Pothonggang Hotel to watch CNN, and we tracked the Arab Spring. Carolyn streamed Obama's speeches for our theoretical eavesdroppers. Even though I had learned some Vietnamese and Hindi during my stays in Hanoi and New Delhi, I could not devote enough attention to the practice of Korean. The teacher was irritatingly opaque about daily life and I could not practice it with everyday people on a daily basis. Fact is, the Koreans discouraged our learning Korean and to this day it is one of my great regrets that I still don't speak it.

In some ways, the most revealing part of the compound were the back buildings. When we arrived in Pyongyang, we understood little of what was typically but informally provided for staff and workers by international organizations – and probably, most work units, in some fashion, in the DPRK. On the other hand, these practices were not-quite official arrangements where the rules of the UN might have collided with internal practices of the system's authorities who dealt with foreigners. Openly acknowledging the needs that the office was supposed to take care of – beyond the legal and transparent HR realm of salaries and entitlements – would have exposed the hardship of the lives of even the most privileged North Koreans, an embarrassment to our handlers and staff. With the scrutiny that came with UNDP's reopening, there was little reason to officialize these 'extras' given questions that could get raised about the propriety of a few of the amenities the office provided. It was in everyone's interest that much was left unsaid.

I was dealing with the work of the UN and UNDP. That kept me more than occupied. Meanwhile, Carolyn was trying to figure out how things worked in Pyongyang, just as she had in our previous postings. Unlike in New York or even post-UNTAC Cambodia or in Delhi during the years of India Shining where home and office were separate domains, and more akin to a then-isolated Hanoi in 1983, Pyongyang was an intimate duty station, as we called our assignments, where your personal life and the workings of the office and the relationships of all the people are intertwined. Such an environment makes for a rich emotional life of connection but would get exhausting and did require judgment about when it was essential to impose boundaries.

Carolyn was immediately curious about the activity in the low-slung, slightly hidden long buildings behind the main office. When someone finally explained, 'This is the cafeteria,' that was helpful and completely normal. It felt to her like what was going on back there was a state secret which of course only piqued her interest. She had some questions about how the cook and food were being financed, given the food rationing system and UNDP's ability to have a cook on staff. But this was completely in the realm of normal.

There were other rooms and structures, however. The one that got Carolyn most distressed was the garage. First of all, she mightily objected to the Audi being the official UN 'Res Rep car' as being wasteful and truly offended her NGO instincts and her generally 'with-the-people' outlook. But then when she found out that the garage for the Audi was heated, while so many in the country suffered without any heat or power in the frigid cold, she was pretty much beyond talking to and disliked that car every time she climbed into it.

The other spaces took a few weeks for her to figure out. She noticed people coming in and out of the back, with wet hair and changed clothes. It looked like it was a bathhouse. There also seemed to be laundry going on. Her first reaction was, well, why is all this going on at the office? People do these chores at home. When she asked me, I hadn't noticed anything as I was absorbed in the front office while she was spending her time noticing the back. She came to realize how important the hot water and facilities were for the staff on a daily basis, with people taking turns during the workday to use the facilities. They did not have hot water at home, or perhaps even running water.

Our discovery and questioning of facility issues must have seemed awkward and full of presumption to the Koreans, and even to long-time expatriate residents who could see our French-American and New Yorker sensibilities come up against the North Korean lifestyle. We are a UN family and spend our lives seeking common values across nationality and the richness of cultural differences to ground the work at hand, but we've always known that we all have our biases. In Pyongyang, it was important that we learned to accept the unofficial ways in which we shored up the lives of the staff and not go around demanding disclosure for everything as an indicator of our commitment to truth and democracy. This may sound like making a mountain out of a molehill at best and self-aggrandizing at worst, but this is how we could sometimes experience our actions and reactions.

A sure bet for fun for the men at the office was anything to do with sports. A volleyball net appeared when our daughter who played college volleyball at her college visited. When I expressed interest in honing my table tennis game, staff members immediately took action. A table was miraculously found that I could personally purchase. Pick up was immediately arranged with a driver and vehicle. And from that point on, the ping pong table would appear in the large entrance foyer of UNDP at lunch and on weekends. I would play regularly with the other office driver, a former table tennis champion. Well, not exactly play. He would make me practice. After one week exclusively hitting forehands, I asked, 'What about practicing backhands?' Next week, was his answer.

Carolyn decided she needed her own car and found a decrepit temporary vehicle, a VW Jetta, through Lee, a Chinese-Korean businessman. It arrived with a red license plate – reserved for foreign private citizens, usually Chinese businessmen. She soon found a set of pale blue UN plates discarded long ago, stashed away in the greenhouse, and switched them out. It was unorthodox to use bogus plates but it got her on the road.

Eventually, the Jetta that was ordered through Lee arrived and driving resumed with proper registration. But one national colleague, perhaps inspired by Carolyn's resourcefulness, and tired of the extra visa paperwork he was tasked to do on account of her US citizenship, proposed listing her as a Chinese citizen to ease the process. I promptly tore up the form when he submitted it to me! Later on, I heard from an American friend with partial Chinese ancestry that he too had been listed as ethnically Chinese by his North Korean hosts.

Carolyn's experience in the DPRK was definitely marked by her status as the only US citizen in residence in Pyongyang. Her nationality quickly became less of a headline as she was afforded the same autonomy as any international expatriate, driving around town in her own car, organizing for the Women's Association, and taking care of our domestic lives. She was also able to help various UN projects and NGOs with short-term projects, consulting for programme evaluations, writing and editing publications, facilitating planning sessions. Her practical activities in Pyongyang were far less controlled than when she was a student in Beijing in 1979-80, or when she was the sole US resident in a then-isolated Hanoi in 1983.

But the overall atmosphere in Pyongyang was exceptionally staged, watched and just plain odd. She would on occasion joke that she was ready to retire from her lifelong tour of Asian despotic regimes to deal with shoring up progressive politics in the United States, where she could actually fully participate, rather than pontificate about other countries over which she would never be a stakeholder. And she was truly upset when the authorities would not give our future daughter-in-law a visa to visit us in Pyongyang with our son, because she was American. After all, Carolyn thought, we had lived in the DPRK for two years and had tried to demonstrate our good intentions at being there. But no. She'd have to come with a tour group. Carolyn's negative reaction –there are many ways to say 'forget you' – made it all the way up the officers within the MFA. They did feel bad but could do nothing about it. In probably one of the most ironic trips ever made by an expatriate based in Pyongyang, Carolyn actually travelled to Seoul as a private citizen (and 2008 Obama delegate) to participate in a Democrats Abroad meeting as the organization prepared for the 2012 US presidential election.

The throughline to Carolyn's DPRK experience was her observations about how ordinary people were dealing with food. She had this worrying feeling that hunger was more than a past memory, that scarcity was a constant preoccupation. It may have been over-sensitivity, but food-related concerns seemed to be everywhere: the mobilizations necessary for harvest, the making of kimchee at the office cafeteria, the Chusok holiday of golden sun (mid-autumn harvest festival in October) as a time of plenty, the measured yet intense management of daily meals, the ration lines, the sad supermarkets, the dour private outdoor markets – determined the seasonality of the country, taking up mental energy of everyone she met. This was how she became interested in gardening, about which she knew nothing.

The problem with this interest was her utter lack of knowledge and experience. She got books about four-season gardening and composting. She saw how other expatriates had nurtured productive gardens on their embassy grounds. She enlisted the help of the UNDP gardener, who it turned out actually knew everything. She brought seeds from China, France and the US. She also brought in 'hose technology' – long, short, drip, nozzles – an improvement over buckets. (The hoses were put to use in many ways beyond watering the garden, mostly to wash cars –the DHL van and other UN agency vehicles would get hosed down in the compound – and once to have a water-sprinkler party for families with young children on a hot summer day.).

With advice and support from our friend at Save The Children UK, the Service Bureau built a wooden two-bin compost system (copied from a New York City promotional brochure). Carolyn read books about composting, tried, made mistakes (I once buried the foulest mixture underground, after her pile turned anaerobic) and eventually succeeded. We would drive all over the diplomatic compound and load yellow, stinky, gingko leaves into the back of the Audi. With cafeteria and household food scraps, the pile would transform into rich, moist, dark, crumbly, earthy-smelling and aerated manure. In the winter, the pile was so warm, reaching 70°C (160°F), I'd see smoke rise outside. Consecration came when officers from the Ministry of Agriculture visited the successful experiment.

We didn't grow enough food to provide for ourselves, which would have taken another couple of seasons, but we did cultivate vegetables and herbs. Like good students, Carolyn and the gardener tried the 'Three Sisters' Native American planting technique, growing beans, corn and squash together in a kind of triplex – which turned out to be better suited to hot and dry climates rather than Pyongyang's cool and wetter environment. Spinach, lettuces, and *bok choy* varieties thrived. The garden produced beautiful Halloween-ready pumpkins, enough basil for an Italian friend to test out many pesto recipes, great green cucumbers. And the flower seeds from the Brooklyn Botanic Garden were spectacular when mixed with the local varieties. However compelling the garden was to her, Carolyn was aware that she was a dilettante compared to the hard labour that the staff had endured in the fields. Sometimes I would give her a hard time, comparing the UNDP compound to Trianon, the garden at Versailles where Marie-Antoinette invited her guests to play just before the French revolution put an end to that lifestyle.

It was natural for Carolyn to notice women cooking in many settings because she has always cooked for our family. She had learned in other countries about the dangers of smoke inhalation from cooking fires, the arduous effort for women to find wood to burn and clean water to drink, and the mortal threat of catching on fire from the flames. She had never before considered the problems of cooking on fire in a cold climate. The cold made it harder to heat anything and was a challenge. She asked a friend in Washington, DC for technical advice (at the time, this was a deep interest of Hillary Clinton) and she managed to find an efficient prototype of a cookstove manufactured in Seoul. She brought in that model to show to experts in the DPRK, in the hopes that this might influence design and eventual production. That the prototype came from Seoul created plenty of buzz. I had seen traditional ondol systems that combine wood-burning stoves and heated beds or floors, but cooking requires a freestanding, efficient stove. This type of technology was key to improving the status of women.

The apricot trees on the office premises yielded lots of fruit suitable for jams and compotes. Carolyn could make a pot of jam at a time but it bothered her that the fruit was rotting on the ground. But then she remembered my sister dumping a clear eau-de-vie liquor into glass jars in the French countryside to make a cherry liqueur and thought we could do the same with the apricots. Once the drivers and staff got wind of the idea, a barrel of soju became available for the project. We basically left a barrel of apricots in the liquor with some cinnamon sticks to ferment in the hallway of the apartment. I don't think we even bothered to remove the pits. The liquor – what Americans call moonshine – was original if a bit rough. And certainly high in alcohol content. We shared it with guests and managed to bring a bottle back to New York, where the brew was deemed original and very rough.

The garden gave us an opening for conversations with Koreans and expatriate experts about farming and food. What gets planted, and how.

What becomes available to harvest and eat, and when. We came to appreciate the special roots, mushrooms and forest edibles prized as delicacies. We had to learn the importance of early spring potatoes in combating seasonal hunger. Watching the gardener toss and sow several pounds of spinach seeds in the cold, late fall so that they would sprout through the frost in the early spring seemed like an act of hope against the fear of scarcity. Carolyn experienced how cut off we in industrialized countries are from the sheer power of nature that helps us survive. She remains grateful to the gardener for quietly and diligently showing her how to grow things.

On weekends, we sought relaxation in simple routines. In winter, we walked through Moran Park. Snow blanketed the hill. The frozen Taedong River glistened below. We spoke quietly through our thick mufflers about the months past and those to come.

Chapter 10

SPROUTS

Expanding the role – Jimmy Carter and former presidents visit – Maternal mortality – An orphanage – One colleague leaves – Back surgery

TRACK II negotiations between the US and North Korea offer a 'dialogue between non-officials of nations designed to make up the perceived shortcomings in the official dialogue', as Former Secretary of Defence William Perry called them. It comprises unofficial contacts, projects and workshops between the DPRK and American think tanks, such as the National Committee on North Korea, Carnegie Corporation and academic institutions. Each of these projects complement the official Six Party Talks and provide a venue for multilateral and bilateral communications when, as is often the case, official negotiations are suspended.

* * *

In early 2011, I feared that DPRK's global relations, especially with the US, might continue to disrupt our efforts. I had seen Pascoe's efforts on behalf of the UN fail to restart a dialogue. When that happened, I became a little less naïve about the tired, unproductive dichotomy between nukes and nutrition. I viewed our persistent efforts to engage with the DPRK as a form of optimism and belief that sustained engagement contained its own value. I had by then abandoned my initial hope of being in the front row when DPRK would change and open up. The goal was more simply to, as someone once told me, 'keep the soup warm'.

I learned quickly that with North Korea, words carried weight far beyond the room they were spoken in. For the UN to be effective, we had to speak with one voice to governments, donors, and anyone else listening. Problems, solutions, and the funding needs for programmes had to be laid out clearly. That meant I had to become conversant in the specifics of many sectors in which I was not expert – agriculture, nutrition, population, disaster preparedness, energy and health – to play the role of an effective advocate.

The UN in the DPRK shouldered tasks that, anywhere else, would fall to sprawling, well-funded institutions. We acted as the essential meeting point for the international community – embassies, NGOs, international organizations, and a handful of individuals doing not-for-profit work. I felt it strategic not only to keep that small community together but to expand the UN's ability to convene it.

Our diplomatic circle was small enough to feel like a club: ten embassies from Asia, seven from the EU, and a scattering from Africa, Latin America, and the Middle East. Palestine had an embassy here, officially recognized by the DPRK. France, which had never formalized ties, still kept a lone representative inside the EU diplomatic building – a quiet signal that engagement could survive even without formal recognition. In such a tight group, personalities mattered. China and Russia most of all played the long game. The Russian Ambassador, a career Korea specialist, could conduct an entire conversation in flawless Korean.

Every Friday, I chaired the Inter-Agency Meeting (IAM) in the UNDP conference room. On paper, it was for information-sharing; in practice, it was part therapy session, part intelligence swap. Diplomats, less frequently allowed beyond Pyongyang than aid workers, relied on them to bring back scraps of reality from the countryside. In return, they fed us the shifting moods of their capitals and the geopolitical undercurrents that could shape our work. It was a quiet barter system, and one well worth managing.

The IAM became a magnet for visitors. If they were lucky enough to be in Pyongyang on a Friday, they would stop by and participate in the meeting. I occasionally invited people from outside the diplomatic area, for example expatriate teaching staff from the Pyongyang University of Science and Technology. The meetings could be safe haven or sparring match: people shared intelligence, grumbled about bureaucratic brick walls, celebrated tiny wins, and dissected the inevitable failures. Afterward, we would drift next door to the Friendship Restaurant, where over kimchi and beer, other deals – less official, no less important – were struck.

My interest in being the international community's 'eyes and ears' extended well beyond the DPRK's borders. The Governments of Japan and South Korea regularly requested briefings, allowing me both to keep the DPRK high on their agendas and to make targeted appeals for funding. I also met with diplomats in Beijing, Seoul, and Geneva who sought deeper insight into conditions inside the country. One particularly productive engagement took place in Washington, D.C., organized by the National Committee on North Korea (NCNK) and the UNDP Washington office. There, I met members of Congress from both parties – including staffers involved in the 2007 UNDP investigation – along with White House officials and policy experts from prominent think tanks. They were keen to hear our most up-to-date assessments of the situation on the ground. In later years, I have taken genuine interest in hearing my successors deliver similar briefings.

In Pyongyang, it was a quiet victory whenever China or Russia – North Korea's two most important partners and fellow members of the Security Council – sent a representative to the IAM. In those moments, I was reminded that our footing in the DPRK didn't rest solely on traditional European and American donors. The balance depended just as much on the goodwill – or at least the attention – of the neighbours who mattered most.

* * *

The expansive role of the UN in the DPRK was exemplified when an organization called The Elders contacted our office. The Elders were an international non-governmental organization founded by Nelson Mandela in 2007. It comprised independent global leaders, including former presidents and other influential figures, who worked together to address global issues. Former President Carter was a member, first among equals. He wanted to return to the DPRK to see what he could do to re-start negotiations centred around the DPRK. He would be accompanied by two former Presidents: Mary Robinson of Ireland and Martti Ahtissari of Finland. I had always held Carter's 1994 intervention in North Korea as a fine example that diplomacy, even using unofficial channels, could be effective in reducing tensions with North Korea. His visit to the DPRK remains one of the most important examples of backchannel diplomacy in modern history. He made an unprecedented visit, with President Clinton's quiet approval, to North Korea amid rising tensions that had escalated to the brink of military conflict over North Korea's nuclear programme. In a series of direct talks with Kim Il Sung, Carter secured North Korea's agreement to freeze its nuclear programme in exchange for negotiations on improved relations with the US. His visit also paved the way for future diplomatic efforts, leading to the Agreed Framework later that year, in which North Korea committed to halting its nuclear weapons development in return for aid and assistance with civilian nuclear energy. Carter's ability to engage Kim Il Sung personally, bypassing the more hostile rhetoric of official US channels, helped shift the situation from a military standoff to diplomatic dialogue.

Jimmy Carter could however not work his magic with Leader Kim Jong Il. Perhaps Kim was already too ill. He did not receive President Carter but asked Minister Kim Gye Gwan to read him a personal message expressing a desire to reduce tension and improve inter-Korean relations, including a summit meeting with President Lee of South Korea.

Carter received a little bit of the old Pyongyang run-around but was too good a politician to show any frustration about it. At least we managed to get out of the city to visit UN projects. I enjoyed the sight of President Carter waving through his minibus' window at confused North Korean pedestrians in the town of Pyongsong, as if from a presidential limousine to his constituents. Once a president, always a president.

* * *

For some time, my UNFPA colleagues had voiced their deep concern about the grim reality of maternal mortality in North Korea. The statistics were not just alarming – they were a stark indictment of the country's long decline. Maternal mortality, perhaps more than any other health indicator, laid bare the extent of the collapse in quality of life compared to North Korea's East Asian neighbours. In 1990, North Korea had been roughly on par with China, Japan, South Korea, and other smaller East Asian nations, with maternal mortality rates (MMR) hovering around 50 deaths per 100,000 live births. But two decades later, the divergence was dramatic. While other East Asian countries had reduced their MMR by about 13 points, North Korea's had climbed by 31 points, reaching 81 per 100,000 births – if not more – according to World Bank estimates. If that figure was even close to accurate, and many experts believed it was, it placed North Korea among the worst-performing health systems in the world.

The country had regressed to a point where childbirth had become an act of survival. The numbers spoke for themselves: this was a public health failure and a damning reflection of the state's disregard for women's lives.

It raised a fundamental question: what exactly were the Ministry of Public Health's priorities for women's health? In contrast to other sectors – where political consensus and bureaucratic will could be quickly mobilized – a picture emerged of chronic neglect. When it came to electrifying a rural household, for instance, there was often broad agreement: villagers, local authorities, and Pyongyang bureaucrats all pushed to move forward. Similarly, when the topic was agricultural development – improving yields through training and new inputs – the government showed no hesitation. But when the issue was the survival of women during pregnancy and childbirth, that resolve evaporated.

There were, of course, dedicated and competent professionals within the Ministry and across hospitals and clinics. They cared deeply. But their commitment was not matched by the system around them. The indifference was not technical – it was political and societal. It reflected a vacuum of leadership where it mattered most. Maternal and infant deaths were not treated as urgent threats. In the eyes of the regime, existential danger came from beyond its borders. And that external threat continued to dictate national priorities, crowding out most others.

The UN agencies – WHO, UNICEF, and UNFPA – alongside the Red Cross and a small number of international NGOs, tried to respond. They brought in expertise, upgraded delivery rooms, and expanded access to emergency obstetric and neonatal care. We trained healthcare workers, supplied essential medicines like oxytocin and magnesium sulphate, and promoted breastfeeding and good nutrition. The UN and NGOs distributed micronutrient supplements and ran rural outreach programmes to equip household doctors, hoping to extend services to even the most remote communities.

But there were limits to what the UN could do. We could not patch the foundational weaknesses of a collapsing health system. If hospitals weren't stocked with drugs, no training or equipment could save a woman hemorrhaging in childbirth. If a woman needed to be transferred to a provincial hospital for emergency care, there was no guarantee she would get there in time – given the lack of ambulances, poor road conditions, numerous security checkpoints, and general transportation breakdowns. The national family planning programme was feeble. Reproductive tract infections were widespread. Cervical cancer was the second most common cancer among women, yet the country lacked basic diagnostic tools for early detection. Adolescent reproductive health didn't even appear on the national agenda.

My colleagues at WHO, UNICEF, and UNFPA worked persistently to convince the Ministry to adopt Maternal Death Reviews – a cornerstone of modern public health that investigates the causes of pregnancy-related deaths to prevent future ones. But the push met stiff resistance. The doctors we engaged, mostly men, were unwilling to participate. At best they deflected; at worst, they stonewalled. The result was predictably frustrating. We hit the same barriers over and over again: lack of data, fragmented information, institutional fear of accountability.

Attempts to raise taboo topics – adolescent pregnancy, sexual violence, unsafe abortion – met with little more success. The truth was stark: teenage girls, single mothers, women in rural areas, or anyone with an unplanned pregnancy had almost no access to quality reproductive health services. Family planning awareness remained low; just 62 per cent of women even knew about the limited contraceptive options available to them, which consisted mostly of intrauterine devices and sterilization.[1] The competence of North Korean health workers could not offset this larger failure. Their discipline and ingenuity were extraordinary. A UN doctor recalls recall leaving behind medical textbooks, only to return and find them thoroughly read, marked up, discussed, and memorized. The talent was there. The dedication was there. But the system did not prioritize the survival of women.

* * *

The reality of the regime's investing in its survival above all else was also apparent in the nation's network of baby home nurseries and orphanages. The orphanage as an institution has largely been sidelined for a generation in industrialized countries as birth rates have declined and foster care and adoption became better alternatives to institutionalization. This is less true in ex-Communist countries. The orphanage and baby home system in the DPRK was an important part of the country's system of caring for the most vulnerable in society, infants and young children. As a result, we would occasionally but regularly visit them.

With the Pyongyang International Women's Group (PIWA) and many colleagues, Carolyn worked intensively with one orphanage in Kaesong over three years in an effort to help the facility and the children it served. Describing the conditions in the orphanages she worked with is difficult. There is no world where an institutionalized baby is a good thing to see. In the DPRK, where food and heat were at a premium for everyone, the orphanages and baby homes were no different. Scarcity was apparent, as was the Sisyphean effort by staff to keep the children fed and warm.

The international women were brought to this particular baby home because it needed help, unlike other facilities in Pyongyang. In Carolyn's view, this pairing of PIWA members with that orphanage was in itself a brave decision because they were shown unwell children in a struggling facility, not a showcase. The orphanage buildings were typical multistorey concrete blocks. Children were grouped by age. There was ample space for sleeping rooms and sometimes separate playrooms. There were often child-friendly paintings on the walls. The rooms were clean. The facilities were bare and austere, without the disorder – or joy – that usually follows young children.

The newborns looked especially undernourished and listless. Some rooms had cribs. Other rooms had traditional thick quilted mattresses on the floor, with babies swaddled in warm and colourful padded blankets. The rooms were quiet. A health expert later explained to the PIWA group that babies cry to get attention and their needs met, but when crying does not bring comfort – or nourishment – babies will go quiet to conserve their energy. The silence of the rooms and hallways was unsettling.

Sometimes PIWA would bring UNICEF measuring tapes to measure the upper arms of the babies, a marker of nutritional status. But as mothers, even without measuring, they could see that these children were not thriving. Carolyn felt solidarity and surprise when the Chinese Ambassador's wife, towards the end of a visit to Kaesong, said with a pained expression, 'The government must take care of their people' in Chinese and then allowed her statement to be translated to our small group. The babies looked malnourished. Many had skin rashes on their faces and heads. Some of the babies had a hard time sitting up, oddly flopping towards the floor. (The group was later told such weakness was due to rickets, caused by lack of Vitamin D and calcium.) The babies weren't trying to wiggle around, or crawl. When Carolyn would hold a baby, he or she would have little affect or response. Older toddlers would sit together in a room, quite still.

Carolyn found these visits disturbing. There are thousands of orphans in the DPRK. Not all lost both parents. Sometimes one or both parents was sent to work to another region or fell ill. It was not clear why extended families could not take in the children as a better option, but the tragedy was in the certain hardship that led to the children's placement. We also had to assume that these children were in a pipeline to military conscription.

The PIWA group would come with questions. How and how much were the children fed? What were they eating? Were there wet nurses? How did these babies wind up at the orphanage? Did family members ever visit the babies? These questions were answered on the margins, over time. But the essential information that PIWA did have was that the facility was very cold in the winter and that the children were not getting enough to eat. She thought that PIWA could make a difference for the children in this one facility, if they got organized.

And then PIWA was 'assigned' – in the mysteriously bureaucratic ways of the authorities dealing with foreigners in Pyongyang – to work directly with the Red Cross Society of the DPRK. During my time in the DPRK, the DPRK Red Cross Society was an active and reliable humanitarian organization. With support from the international Red Cross and Red Crescent movement, and like many Red Cross organizations worldwide, the Red Cross in the DPRK actively supported flood relief efforts, addressing issues like water supply, infrastructure damage, and food aid, provided first aid training to the public, contributing to emergency preparedness. In the DPRK, they implemented healthcare programmes, particularly for women and children, and organised large-scale tree-planting projects to reduce landslides and flooding.

The PIWA–Red Cross connection turned into a useful partnership and created a truly mutual opportunity to make tangible things better at one orphanage. The Kaesong facility had needs and was open to PIWA's help, and there seemed a few tracks to assist the Kaesong orphanage.

The obvious challenge was to find ways to help nourish the children. Hunger lurks around many corners in the DPRK. The fear of it, the managing away from it, though unspoken felt ever present, just below the surface. Carolyn and her colleagues always assumed this came from widespread suffering during famine times along with seasonal shortages during the lean early spring and bad harvests or other ongoing shocks to the food supply.

Though the women's group became quickly aware of the problem of adequate feedings for the infants and young children, the 'how' took time to figure out and then implement. In her many visits to schools, workplaces and baby homes, Carolyn never saw a functioning kitchen or cafeteria with actual meal preparation underway, or children or staff eating. This reinforced her perception of scarcity and the ever-unsaid preoccupation with food – and the complexity of how to improve things.

An immediate way PIWA could help would be to purchase infant formula in China for the youngest of the babies. Reservations about this were expressed because it was not sustainable – PIWA would not be able to buy enough formula forever – and they wanted to make sure the formula stayed with the orphanage babies and not wind up on the black market. But after some discussion among the group, they realized that whatever could be done as a volunteer in-country group was probably by definition not all that sustainable, so they shouldn't get paralysed from taking action. The children needed immediate calories. The group termed the infant formula as supplemental to whatever they were already getting and negotiated with the orphanage that they monitor and report regularly – in the same way as more official feeding projects required – regularly recorded weight and arm circumference improvements for each baby.

Another track for PIWA's intervention was to expose the children to sunshine which would help them cope with the long winter cold, as well as boost Vitamin D exposure to reduce the risk of rickets. The orphanage director and Red Cross leadership suggested that a winterized sunroom could be added to the front of the facility so that the children could get sun. As the build would resemble a greenhouse, which the Koreans were familiar with, and because a PIWA member was an Italian architect, they managed to design, order and import the building materials from China, and get it built locally on site.

PIWA researched the work of international NGOs and UN programmes and found that soybean milk can be reasonably tolerated by very young infants, and soybean milk processing relies on a fairly simple machine that could be imported from China. Other group homes had been using the same machines, or so they heard through the grapevine. PIWA arranged for a study tour from the Kaesong orphanage to a place that had the machine, so that they could learn how to operate and maintain it. The staff benefited from seeing another facility's operation, and they probably discussed backstory problems such as how to cajole up soybeans from the system. PIWA also provided a generator, durable stainless-steel trays, sieves and pots so that the orphanage could produce tofu to eat or sell, in addition to soy milk.

Finally, there was the idea of giving the orphanage a way to earn income or produce something of value, to provide a stream of income above the most basic of rations, get them through lean times, and create a sliver of autonomy. PIWA tried this with the soybean machine, which could be used to directly feed the children but also to generate income through the sale of excess tofu. Given the extreme poverty in the DPRK and the lack of transport options for most of the population, another less orthodox way was to get them a vehicle – a motorbike with a cart – to use for their own needs but also to leverage, barter and earn for needed commodities. PIWA learned from Korean and expatriate friends working with NGOs that the ownership of equipment could raise issues for the orphanage, so PIWA retained ownership and leased out the soybean machine and the motorcycle cart. We reasoned that if PIWA owned the assets, no other organization or entity could take the equipment away from the orphanage. It was a kind of insurance policy.

Figure 10.1 Carolyn negotiates deliveries with the Red Cross, Kaesong City. Photo by Jerome Sauvage.

PIWA needed money to purchase these materials and needed help from the international community to bring in goods from Dandong, China. Dandong could be reached by car from Pyongyang and expats would visit to get provisions and recharge from the stress of the DPRK. Plus, once a year, we had to take the fancy Audi to China for maintenance!

Dandong brought us back into the modern age without our forgetting our proximity to North Korea. Modern high-rises rose above the Yalu River. The border post felt anachronistic. From our hotel window we could see piles of goods being loaded into vans and trucks clogging the Friendship Bridge (the new bridge was not built as yet). Trains carrying grain and coal into the DPRK seemed to us to be a lifeline for the DPRK. Enterprising Chinese hawkers showed statues commemorating the war during which Mao's son was killed. Local guides took tourists boating on the Yalu while reminding them that it was forbidden to give food to North Koreans from the boat, I saw a young North Korean boy shouting at us, gesturing for us to give him something to eat. Part of the visit would be to bring back buckets of Kentucky Fried Chicken to our North Korean drivers who were waiting for us on the other side.

The outgoing chair of PIWA was the wife of the Iranian ambassador. There seemed to be euros that belonged to PIWA from previous years, though it was a bit unclear exactly how much and who had access. Carolyn did not think those Euros should be used for PIWA members to take trips to Dandong or otherwise socialize, which apparently had been done in the past.

I was getting concerned that Carolyn was going to get into a tiff with her Iranian colleague. A pointed disagreement did come up but between an Indonesian and the Iranian member, thankfully without Carolyn's involvement. She was able to get most of the Euros out of the Iranian embassy and into an envelope held by the finance officer of a UN agency who volunteered for PIWA as treasurer, and onto a spreadsheet for the international community to see. Carolyn suspected that some members were using PIWA's euros as hard currency they needed when visiting China, and as things moved forward, she and others managed the euros on behalf of PIWA's charitable aims, and wrote a regular newsletter that included a financial report.

But beyond the old stash of euros, new funding was needed to meet the needs of the orphanage. PIWA resurrected a community fair that had been done in years past, with each embassy or organization cooking their national dishes to sell, and an auction of donations from the many countries. Script money was introduced to lessen the circulation of cash so that proceeds really would go to the orphanage with a minimum of leakage, and the PIWA group leaned on everyone to participate. The group organized three fairs while we were in Pyongyang, and raised thousands of euros during the period we were there. Arabs from Syria and Egypt, South Asians from India, Iran, Nepal and Pakistan, southeast Asia members of ASEAN and countries from the European Union, Chinese, Russians and UN agencies participated. As most had their flag and national dress on display at the fairs, Carolyn did manage to put an American flag out next to her cookie tray, which was strategically placed on one side of the Canadian NGO table, though her Polish friend with Cold War memories was doubtful that was such a great idea. A young Chinese journalist from Xinhua news agency asked for an explanation of the flip charts on the wall. She was interested that PIWA would post an itemized account of PIWA expenses and the exact costs of what they would purchase for the orphanage in full public view. Carolyn described her approach to transparency, that the money being raised that day belonged to the orphanage, and that every person participating had a right to see how the money would be used.

With the money raised, when international friends would go on personal trips to Dandong or Beijing they would buy on our behalf and bring back baby formula, diapers, warm clothing (and sanitary napkins for the all-female staff of the orphanage). We would work with Lee, the Chinese trader, to order building materials, the soybean machine equipment, and later a motorcycle-powered cart as ostensibly our personal items in order to clear customs. (UNDP colleagues and probably the next level authorities knew what we were doing but by then we thought they trusted that PIWA would deliver all the goods to the orphanage so never gave PIWA a hard time.)

The two PIWA co-chairs at the time, Carolyn and her friend the wife of the UNICEF Representative would ask UNICEF, UNDP and WFP for trucks and drivers to deliver goods to Kaesong (and to deal with the necessary clearances). Carolyn would throw in gunny sacks of half-cooked compost from the UNDP pile along with pounds of spinach and vegetable seeds (from China, the US, or South Korea) that the orphanage could use at their collective farm or vegetable plot. PIWA members collected clothing, biscuits, rice, soybeans, bar soap, detergent, fresh oranges or apples to be sent to Kaesong via truck or when we would visit in UN or embassy vehicles.

This work kept Carolyn going in Pyongyang. It took three years, resolving big and small problems as she learned the system, and was made a success by Koreans and internationals who eased the back channels to allow for a range of activities and who offered wise counsel and generous material support. She formed a close working relationship with the Director of the International Department of the Red Cross who facilitated many aspects of the work and provided practical suggestions. She made friends with many PIWA women.

Carolyn also knew how subversive the PIWA's activities and fundraising fairs were – truly voluntary, community-wide celebrations with common purpose among a motley group of expatriates who found themselves together only because their countries chose or were allowed to have official representation to the DPRK. It had the look and feel of a family, charitable event anywhere, and somehow that was going to be just very challenging to the way things were done in Pyongyang. For all the fervency of patriotism in the DPRK, this value did not extend to allowing people to decide to do something together on their own for anything in the public sphere if it was not officially sanctioned. People were told in their work or residential units what was to be done collectively, and then those directives were followed. As far as we could see, there was little or no room for initiative that would engage or organize outside official channels.

For the first two years, the powers that be had allowed local staff of WFP and UNDP to help with the logistics of the fundraiser, even allowing a few Korean staff inside the grounds and building where it was held on the weekend. But by the third year, when the event was big, the money raised significant and non-profit norms established, the word came down that no local staff would be allowed near the event. As the authorities did not have to justify their actions to us, we never knew the official reasons, only that the two or three people who could have helped would not be coming. Carolyn assumed that the open spirit of the event whose success required groups to self-organize and cooperate, and the way we handled money that in its transparency held us accountable – were not considered good influences by the authorities. What were they afraid of? It was actually a day of fun! Food, games, artisanal items from each country, a rummage sale (consisting of old office furniture and an honours-system cash box), raffles – put together through shared effort to raise money for a good cause. It was actually a shock that this could rise to the level of discussion somewhere in the bureaucracy that minded us. Carolyn took their misplaced concern as a soft power victory. And the funding raised made everything possible at the orphanage. She heard a few years after our departure that the

Figure 10.2 Orphanage boy in sunroom. Photo by Carolyn Sauvage-Mar.

Kaesong orphanage was doing well because of PIWA's assistance, and that PIWA's women had started to work with a different facility.

* * *

That spring, Carolyn's hard work with the gardener brought the garden back to life. The garden was magical. In the front, amid field flowers, huge sunflowers gyrated curiously, bringing a note of fantasy in a place devoid of it. When summer arrived, we harvested and prepared the garden's bounty: beans, lettuce, tomatoes, cucumber, enormous squashes, pumpkin. Sadly, I heard that after we left North Korea, the gardener was removed, and the garden was abandoned. Why this waste, I never could understand nor accept. I used to think leadership came from above, from resolutions and memoranda. But in Pyongyang, I'd begun to learn that change – if it came at all – emerged like Carolyn's sprouts: tentative, slow, sometimes invisible to those who demanded loud declarations.

* * *

One Sunday morning in the spring, we took our bicycles for a long day ride. We would pass grass dividers in front of apartment buildings with people kneeling and cutting tiny onions, boys in Army fatigues whitewashing walls, as if preparing a casern for inspection, a few older ladies crouching on their heels or sitting on plastic coolers. A young woman's blue dress gave out a splash of colour amidst the dull brown and green clothing. A few blocks further, I saw the same exact dress on another woman. Recent shipment from China!

We rode by a huge monument where stood, tower-like, a hammer, a sickle, and a writing brush, which represented the alliance of workers, peasants, and intellectuals. From here, large vistas opened up across the river in a well-designed plan, not unlike a bridge over the river Thames.

Within half an hour, we would be out of town. Of the several lovely rides we could take out of the city, riding West towards Nampo or South after crossing the Taedongang river were our favourites. Sunday traffic was even lighter than normal and we'd ride alone on wide, empty highways, crossing occasional bicycle riders or pedestrians. After a few kilometres, we'd turn onto a small road and we'd start along rice fields, alternatively golden or green depending on the season. Sometimes we'd climbed by foot to a hill from which we could see Pyongyang. We once met a teenage boy looking like he lived outdoors, who asked us for food.

On another occasion, walking down from a viewpoint, we came across a group who were relaxing on blankets, some with snacks and drinks. I was glad to see them and waved. They waved back. One man gestured for us to come closer, at the same time walking over to us, jovial and tipsy, his face red from drinking. He wanted to sing a song. His companions laughed nervously. The man paused, stood erect, seized my hand, and took a deep breath before launching into a song. His voice was raw, unguarded, trembling. Between gasps, his face streaked with tears, I thought I heard amid his bellows the name of the North Korean Leader. Around him, his companions stiffened. They weren't just embarrassed – they were anxious. Before he could finish, they closed in, murmuring, urging us to move along.

As we walked away, Carolyn shook her head. 'Who gets brought to tears singing about a country's leader?'

I teased her, 'In the US, you guys did that for Obama . . .'

'We didn't have to get drunk first! And anyway, the song wasn't official, it was 'Yes We Can' by Will I Am!' she retorted, ever the American.

But as we walked on, I couldn't shake the emotions of what we'd just witnessed. Was that man's drunken outburst an act of devotion or defiance? His emotions felt tangled – adoration, yes, but also something else. A frustration that only surfaced when alcohol dulled the fear. And that was what impressed me the most: in North Korea, even love for the Leader could be laced with anguish, and even anguish could not openly be named.

* * *

That spring, sciatica pain in my back became intolerable. I could not feel my toe anymore. The staff at Friendship Hospital in Pyongyang tried all the manipulations possible until they made me understand that they could not help any more than what they'd already tried. The hospital was in a way typical of North Korea: its personnel was motivated and trying very hard, the place kept meticulously clean but it lacked pain-killing medicine and any necessary modern equipment for scanning, such as a magnetic resonance imaging (MRI) scanner, which I was able to find relatively easily at the Military Hospital in Beijing. Within a few weeks I underwent surgery in Hong Kong and quickly fully recovered.

When I returned, one of our colleagues in the office came to see me. She was dynamic and decisive, enjoyed learning, discovering a new world made of equal participation in decision-making, equal access to resources and opportunities, and equal benefits from programmes and projects. I was saddened by her news. The Government had reassigned her husband to another city in North Korea. She had to follow him. She said she tried to stay, had objected that it was not fair that women's careers were subordinated to that of their husbands, but there was nothing she could do. I had enjoyed working with her and she had been among the first persons in this office. We intervened with the Government and managed to keep her a few more months but in the end, she had to go. On her last day, I said, 'at least, we will keep in touch, yes?' She looked at me. I still didn't get it! She tried to remain matter of fact when she said, 'No. We will probably never communicate again.' And indeed, so far, we never did.

Chapter 11

FLOODS AND PARADES

International emergency response – Performances and parades – Kimchi in the office

Protagonists in North Korean fictionalized history show readers the value of their suffering and fates. They transform fear into anger at their enemies, such as Japan and America. Starvation is portrayed as an ordeal that leads the characters in novels to death, but Kim Jong Il's vision of the nation's bright future transforms the protagonists' fear into bliss. Most importantly, the mix of adoration and fear is changed into a sublime and religious experience. The protagonists successfully suppress their fear of death and are willing to die as martyrs for the nation and their leader.[1]

* * *

In the summer, I accompanied a UN humanitarian official to Chongjin in North Hamgyong Province. He administered the UN Emergency Resource Facility from New York, and, as such, represented our largest funder. We would be just one car, Mr Choe, myself and the two visitors. On North Korea's poor road system, it took us two days to drive the 750 kilometres from Pyongyang to Chongjin, only stopping for the night. We reached close to the northern tip of North Korea. We visited hospitals and food distribution centres along the way and met City administrators. We slept in Tanchon, north of Hamhung, and we left the town early in the morning to visit a WFP-supported food factory in Hamhung, South Hamgyong Province, 125 kilometres north of Wonsan. We planned to visit the factory and then return to spend the night in Wonsan.

As we arrived to Hamhung, a heavy rain began. Clouds the colour of lead ran over the edge of roofs, and the light was so faint it felt like five in the afternoon. Pedestrians walked with rounded backs. The North Korean factory staff said that we should visit the factory quickly in order to give ourselves plenty of time to reach Wonsan. The rainstorm could become more threatening, they said.

The factory manager was a German man whom I had never met before and had worked for WFP around the world. His assignment there was temporary and I never had time to chat with him. We were shown through a spotless series of large aluminium vats where they prepared fortified biscuits and a sort of porridge to augment supplies delivered by WFP. Every school child and mother receiving Public Distribution knew of these and we heard that they were popular among the population. This supplement improved nutrition for over two million people, mainly children and pregnant or breastfeeding women in 87 counties.

'How do you know the food isn't being diverted,' I asked?

'Our monitoring system,' the international manager answered, 'tracks each cereal bag from the ship it arrived in, to each of the factories where it is being transformed. We know exactly what amounts of food go to what factory for transformation, and when, down to a single bag of cereal.'

We sat down to eat an individual omelette wrap prepared by the hotel staff in the morning and taken with us on the road, when the North Korean factory manager entered the room and rapidly spoke to Choe. Choe walked over to us.

'We must return to Wonsan now. The storm threatens to turn into a typhoon.'

'Shouldn't we just stay here in Hamhung,' I asked.

'If we leave now we will be okay. It is still early. We will go according to plan.'

The North Korean factory managers were insistent: we needed to leave for Wonsan immediately. I hesitated. The sky had turned into a bruised, seething mass, and the wind began to cut sharply through the air. Something about the urgency in their voices unsettled me.

I frowned. 'Do we have meteorological info? A storm warning?'

The question hung there, useless. Of course, we didn't. North Korea's isolation prevented access to global weather warnings, relying instead on crude, outdated forecasting methods. And no call had come from Pyongyang, so the decision fell on us and we decided to go.

The coast from Hamhung to Wonsan goes South along National Highway 7, partly across a flood plains. These alluvial plains are formed by many tributaries sloping down the hills to the sea, a mile or two away. Hills are partly deforested by people needing fuel to cook and warm their homes, raising the risk of rainwater rushing down the hills. On the other side of the road was the sea. Where the road travels along the plain, it never rises above sea level more than a dozen feet.

Fifteen minutes south of Hamhung, the highway deteriorated into packed dirt, and the storm escalated. The rain attacked the windshield in horizontal sheets, and the wind howled. Pak locked the four-wheel drive and navigated through water pooling across the road.

'This is characteristic of our East Coast,' Choe said, raising his voice over the storm. 'Flooding can occur in one valley and leave the next untouched.'

The road ahead sometimes vanished under water. The SUV slowly moved forward while Choe warned our driver Pak when we drifted too close to the road's edge. No driver should ever attempt to cross a flooded road – but here we were. If the water lifted us even slightly, we could be at the mercy of the current. We heard the sound of rushing water beneath us, but the wheels found grip and we surged forward on the road.

Figure 11.1 Driving in a rainstorm, north of Wonsan City. Photo by Jerome Sauvage.

* * *

By the time we reached Wonsan, other parts of the country, farther west, had experienced more serious flooding. The storm mostly affected the southwest of the country, leaving us in the east mostly unscathed. In North and South Hwangae Provinces and in South Hamyong Provinces, a quarter of the annual rainfall had fallen in five days. Thousands of hectares of rice paddy were submerged; houses and public facilities were destroyed. Casualties were reported although we did not have exact numbers as yet. The Government asked the UN for help.

Back in Pyongyang, I joined in the call for the international community's response. Because the UN, NGOs, the Red Cross and a few bilateral programmes such as Switzerland were already in place in the DPRK, we were able to immediately provide three important and simultaneous services to North Korea and to the international community. First, we sent a damage assessment team comprised of UN teams, the NGO Save the Children International and the International Red Cross. Second, we released pre-positioned stocks for the flood-affected areas, mostly emergency relief kits each containing tarpaulins, blankets, cooking sets and jerry cans as well as oral rehydration tablets, water purification kits, soap, emergency educational kits for children and household doctor bags. And finally we reported news on the situation to the world.[2]

Thankfully, these floods did not devastate as much property or human lives as in previous years. Yet even relatively minor events revealed that North Korea was essentially always vulnerable to weather events. For example, most families relied on shallow dug wells and hand pumps. There was no clear water available in the country to distribute. Dirty groundwater would inevitably increase diarrheal cases. Poorly built constructions that would have stood in other countries were easily swept away by continuous rain.

Agriculture suffered the most. That summer, a series of negative weather events occurred that, once again, demonstrated North Korean agriculture's vulnerability to weather. Heavy cloud cover and rainfall for 60 continuous days from late-June slowed down crop growth because of lack of sunlight. Flooded and waterlogged rice areas were inundated for more than seven days causing the death of rice plants, and maize roots were destroyed from lack of aeration. Typhoons in August coincided with the pollination period of some of the rice and most of the maize with winds high and prolonged enough to severely reduce pollination.

These events were more severe in North Korea's 'rice bowl' in the south of the country, which produced 80 per cent of the nation's cereals. Such localized weather events would create a national crisis.[3]

The year before, torrential rains and floods that hit the DPRK and China from the end of May until August caused the Yalu River to exceed its annual high levels. The Yalu River overflowed from more than 300 mm overnight rainfall in areas around Lake Suphung and heavy rains in border areas of China, triggering heavy floods that submerged much of the city of Sinuiju in North Phyongan Province, causing extensive property losses.[4] In my three years in the DPRK, I only saw one year without catastrophic floods. Floods occurred twice in 2010 (May and August), once in 2011 (July) and once again after my departure in 2013 (May).

In the more mountainous areas (comprising 80 per cent of the land), local communities experienced flash floods on a regular basis. The hills I'd crossed between Chongjin and Wonsan were typical of this landscape and I saw how fast the water ran down the hills towards the sea. Such incidents could damage villages yet rarely came to our attention. We resolved to join other organizations to launch disaster preparedness projects, including early warning systems to help these local communities better protect themselves.

* * *

Disasters like these floods and their emergency responses tend to bring communities of humanitarian workers closer together. North Korea was no exception. Assignments to countries like North Korea may see a faster rotation of expatriate personnel than in easier countries but make relationships quicker to develop and sometimes more intensely felt. Plus, we all lived within a radius of two kilometres of each other.

Pyongyang offered sparse but at times memorable entertainment. We attended occasional concerts, such as a grandiose *Eugene Onegin* from Tchaikovsky, delivered by the State Symphony Orchestra of the DPRK. The Orchestra played at the East Pyongyang Grand Theatre where, a few years earlier, the New York Philharmonic had given a performance that was broadcast around the world. The musician's skills were impressive. I sometimes thought the performances were somewhat mechanical like when the violins' bows always seemed to move up and down in perfect unison.

Among the performances that we attended, three were distinctly North Korean: Arirang, the military parades and an anti-US extravaganza.

The world-famous Arirang Mass Games, named after *Arirang*, the traditional Korean folk song, serve as a dramatic showcase of North Korean history, ideology, and national pride. In this grand gymnastics and artistic performance in a giant stadium in Pyongyang, tens of thousands of gymnasts, dancers, acrobats, and martial artists move in perfect synchronization, forming intricate patterns and symbols that often depict scenes from Korean history, revolutionary struggles, and the leadership of the Kim dynasty. We saw a massive human mosaic by thousands of schoolchildren holding coloured flipbooks, changing pages in perfect unison to create a dynamic, ever-shifting backdrop of patriotic imagery and propaganda messages. It was breathtaking in its scale and precision. Through the year we would notice groups of adults and teenagers practice in open spaces.

One evening, we heard a low rumble on the main road outside the diplomatic enclave. After thirty minutes, the sound hadn't stopped. What could that be? We stepped out of the apartment to find out. The fall night was fair with stars in the sky. A few streetlamps illuminated the main road, highlighting the spectacle unfolding. Hundreds of Army tanks and motorized equipment were entering Pyongyang. Young men with helmets and goggles around their necks stood proudly through the turret next to mounted machine guns, looking far ahead. Enthusiasts came outside of their buildings and waved at them. I remembered that we were due to see a parade the next day when North Korea celebrated the founding of the Korean Workers Party. The performing troops and assets were being moved for the big show.

Many holidays were also organized as mass events in neighbourhoods, often in front of one of the many grand portraits of one or the other Leaders Kim. Lines of children would form, waiting to get a goody bag, gathered under the beatific image of the Leader, a kind of Santa Claus figure. On weekends we would see people walking purposefully to join others somewhere in town, holding what looked like inoperable, old toy wooden rifles. We guessed they were going to practice looking like soldiers for a show or going to actually practice to be soldiers. During periods of preparation, people would sometimes be on their way to practice with plastic flowers in hand – an odd, but recognizable prop. And in rural areas we would see the ubiquitous fire engine red, inspirational slogans painted on the walls of villages as we would drive past.

We went to the KWP anniversary parade. We were driven past Kim Il Sung square, the one with the gigantic portraits of Marx and Engels, where the MFA stood. Ushers directed us to the huge building facing the square and motioned us up the steps to stand at a predesignated level. The fully-armed soldiers here were much taller and fitter than those I had seen so far.

A few hundred foreigners of various nationalities were made to stand on an overhang jutting out like an enormous terrace over the vast plaza. I noticed that the foreign press had been invited and had flown in from Beijing and other nearby locations. Everyone was standing, shuffling, wrapped in warm coats and hats. To our left and right on the terraces, North Koreans also gathered, separated from foreigners by a rope or a staircase. The men wore jackets and ties, the women looked good in traditional Korean *hanbok*. They all wore their red badge over their heart indicating their good Party membership standing. A wider terrace hanged above our head, its low-running parapet covered with a red cloth running the length of the building, which is to say many hundreds of yards. I nodded to a few of the expatriates, then looked down over the plaza.

At our feet, a huge crowd stood, strictly aligned in a dozen large rectangles of thousands of people. Absolutely silent. Behind the crowd, the riverbanks, and beyond, Juche Tower, the symbol of the Juche Idea, the philosophy that Kim Il Sung created. Juche embodies the founding idea of a self-reliant State that independently determines its political, economic, and military affairs. When Carolyn discovered one night that the Juche Tower was lit with a tall red torch, the only light in a dark night, she called it the eye of Mordor in reference to the Dark Tower in the Lord of the Ring. The name stuck in our family. Down on the plaza, everything was symmetrical. Absolutely nothing and no one moved. Formations made of thousands of human beings waiting long minutes in perfect silence and stillness. I wondered how a crowd could be so disciplined.

All at once, these tens of thousands of people started shouting as if an electric current had coursed through the crowd's brain at the same exact instant. They screamed at the top of their lungs, shaking red paper flowers, clapping for perhaps one minute and then stopped at the exact same time. After that, speeches and slogans reverberated around the square with always the same message.

'Great Leader Kim Il Sung is our Father, and General Kim Jong Il is our tender and loving Leader who inspires spontaneous love.'

Then another silence. Then again the same electrical pulse, the same noise, even louder, and, this time, unending. Loudspeakers exploded in a deafening sound, booming inexorably the same four low notes. Boom-Boom-BAAM-Boom. Boom-Boom-BAAM-Boom. Everyone turned up their convulsed screaming faces toward the balcony above our heads. Kim Jong Il appeared, waved for perhaps 5 minutes, and disappeared. But the deafening noise continued for long minutes. The military parade began. Trucks bearing missiles, soldiers goose-stepping. The crowd at our feet moved hundreds of thousands of pieces of cardboards over their heads in perfect unison, forming gigantic billboards. This was Pyongyang, 'the new Rome', the new Eternal City, and the centre of a new civilization, created in the image of Kim Jong Il as a pious, virtuous, and courageous leader or Wise Man. The images would make it to every radio, every TV across the land. Pyongyang had fulfilled its role of showcase to the country. I left the show physically and mentally exhausted.

We also saw performances of a darker tone, far from the orchestrated brilliance and tightly synchronized celebration of power of the famous Arirang games. One such event was the theatrical extravaganza of Broadway proportions directed against the USA. While my French nationality and training somewhat distanced me from reacting to the performance, Carolyn admitted having a hard time sitting through the experience. The show was full of caricature. A band of young women in tight short skirts played deafeningly loud rock music whilst a film portrayed attacks against US troops to excite the audience. There were references to the Korean War, to the seizure of the US Navy intelligence ship USS Pueblo in 1968. With years living abroad and a healthy scepticism of some of the US' foreign policy goals, Carolyn thought herself inoculated against such shows of anti-Americanism and justifiable differences in political views. This was not her first experience, and her distress at the intensity of the propaganda was proof of the intensity of the performance. Several diplomats and expatriates went to see her afterwards to make sure she was alright!

My most difficult instance of propaganda under the cover of art occurred when a spectacle collided with childhood innocence – when political propaganda slipped into playtime. The performance placed children in a violent dramatized situation. It was an official visit to a children's home and the staff had prepared an event for us. Mr Pak stopped the car by a children's playground, surrounded by nursery-style murals of little girls with teddy bear faces, dressed as North Korean soldiers and operating cannons that spewed red tracer bullets toward American military aircraft. The juxtaposition unsettled me, not just because a silent lesson in war took place in a space reserved for children, but because the painting displayed such innocent candour next to a war scene. What did these children see when they looked at this? I tried to imagine my own children growing up with these images, absorbing them before even knowing the meaning of war. Would they have questioned them? Or would they, like these boys, have learned to salute without hesitation?

Inside the school, a poster of a young woman welcomed visitors, teachers and students with her index finger over her mouth as if to shush children passing by her. She was wearing a *hanbok*, the traditional Korean garment, consisting of a yellow and red top joined to a long, full skirt with a looped bow and multi-coloured stripes on the sleeves. Her instructions were exceedingly successful: the whole building was quiet.

We were ushered into a large room where another mural showed rockets launched into the pale blue sky in a cloudy hail of pink flowers. Six little boys looking around seven years old awaited us, looking nervously towards their teachers. Each wore white dance tights, turquoise blue shorts, a white shirt and a crown of laurel leaves on their heads. And each brandished a toy gun. A staff member turned on a portable stereo and loud military-sounding music started. TA-TA-TA. TA-TA-TA. The boys started a choreographed dance. It was mesmerizing.

The boys seemed to be overtaking an enemy fort, rolling on the floor to avoid enemy fire and shooting their guns with both hands in the purest 'special forces' style. The dance lasted about five minutes and while the practice and impressive skills of these young boys was admirable, they did not crack a smile and looked intimidated by the situation. I stepped out into the late afternoon light, unable to process what I'd seen. This was a far cry from the school performances that I had seen and enjoyed elsewhere, when the spontaneity of young children far overshadowed the mastery of the performance. It was disturbing to me to see these children disciplined into a performative perfection. Given the enormous challenges of the country to adequately nourish and educate its young, it was impossible for me to justify the resources poured into these special schools whose purpose was also to prepare and train performers to carry out the propaganda and spectacle needs of the government. I knew UNICEF would make formal complaints to the Government when children were made to march in military parades. But with this small school, a protest wouldn't change anything. The problem was far larger than this one performance.

Experiences like the ones I have just described weighed heavily, even as we found ways to hold onto a sense of normalcy. In a place shaped by control and silence, we tried to find ways to balance our experience, to recognize the ordinary humanity of people we met or observed. And we needed to appreciate North Korea for itself, as we did in every other country we had lived in. One special part of the country is the beauty of the landscape. Sparsely populated compared to the rest of East Asia, the countryside was bucolic and peaceful, a pleasure to drive or bike through. Forested hills offered vistas and hikes with four beautifully different seasons. Mountain peaks formed interesting ranges; a group of us chartered a plane to visit Mt. Chilbo. And the coastline was dramatic, empty of development except for an occasional fishing village.

* * *

Time in Pyongyang had a strange elasticity – days dragging, months vanishing. And then, somehow, the year turned. One morning in the fall, a huge pile of fresh cabbage arrived in front of our office. Everyone joined forces to help the cafeteria cook and the cleaning staff to prepare kimchi for the year. Quantities of salt and coarsely ground red chili powder that provided the characteristic colour and flavour to kimchi, covered the cabbage and spilled to the floor and walls. The whole room was red! They filled vats and buried them underground, which was warmer than the frigid air, to be eaten throughout the year.

We welcomed another annual Crop and Food Assessment. This time, the team gained better access to markets.[5] They were also able to visit homes and farms although they didn't publicize it. They would stop their car at random and check up on any crop or any person, unannounced and unrestrained. They'd visit peoples' homes. They produced better records.

This more successful food assessment constituted proof that persistent presence in the country was the most likely to bear results. I like to use the metaphor that after you pried the door ajar, you worked your darndest to open the window.

Chapter 12

WHOSE VOICE?

Duties and bullies – The Millennium Development Goals Report – Addressing criticisms on human rights

In his dissertation on Kim Jong Il and religious imagination in North Korean literature, scholar Sunghee Kim explains how Kim Jong Il made labour an 'absolute end' by attaching sanctity to its purpose. In so doing, he explains, labour is sublimated to a sacred practice for the sake of '*choguk*' (father country), '*inmin*' (people), '*sahoe*' (society) and '*chiptan*' (commune). This 'most sublime duty' is what the warrior Kim Namch'ŏl's voice within tells him, in Kim Jong Il's biography, *Taking up Guns and Bayonets*. On April 18, 1978, the North Korean socialist state promulgated *Sahoejuŭi rodongpŏp* (Socialist Labor Law). In it, the DPRK stipulates the concept of labour as 'a sacred duty'. By so doing, it prohibits doubts about the worker's sacred vocation. In this way, labour – physical conduct – is transformed into a religious and spiritual practice, and 'loving to work' is celebrated as the people's virtue.[1]

* * *

Observing life inside North Korea presented me with a challenge – not because the truth is hard to see, but because it's easy to misinterpret. Like anyone, I brought to the experience my values, morality, cultural expectations and most likely a Western European bias. What I saw, and then what I tried to make happen in the DPRK, seems uniquely hard to interpret and describe in a way that's fair when it comes to cultural assumptions. At its best, the UN respects cultures and sovereignty. But the denial of so many rights in the DPRK along with the knowledge that (perhaps unwittingly) our colleagues acquiesced and abetted the system showed the limits of our values in practice. A friend of mine told me that what best helped him understand what he saw in the DPRK was literature from all over the world. Carolyn responded to the environment by relying on her belief of the values of democracy contained in the UN Universal Declaration of Human Rights and the Constitution of the United States, which includes the Bill of Rights. She would leave these publications on our coffee tables in whatever country we were living, thinking somehow this appeared subtle rather than hegemonistic. She probably didn't fool anyone, ever, about her politics. But the weirdness of the environment provoked these reactions. Later, when we left definitively, it was in character when she left behind her English-language books on a shelf in an unlocked hallway of the residence building, open to anyone passing by, and slid these missives among the other books thinking, who knows who might read them?

The Korean notion of rights and of duty are deeply imbedded in tradition and culture, supercharged and amplified as propaganda by the regime. While there is often a kernel of truth in propaganda and manipulation, the intent – and effect – is to confuse and then weaponize the information. Then there is the more ambiguous terrain when rights are pretty much ignored in the DPRK in favour of overwhelming pressure towards duty as a value in itself. I came to often and grudgingly admire duty when I would see it operating in the people around me – it seemed as if the people's sense of duty was shaped by the hard realities of necessity, loyalty and endurance.

I was occasionally confronted by people around the world who rightly questioned our UN presence and decried our role in aiding the country to repress and control. My response was that it was just as vital to recognize that the UN supported the dignity of those who continued to care for and serve their people. There were even a few with whom we worked, who tried to subtly open spaces for more open human and honest communication, with whatever risky outcome their honesty might lead to. And then there were the majority who were just trying to get by, do their duty, and who could not be blamed for their efforts to survive.

Coercion was relatively easy to see on display. Once on Munsu Street, near our apartment, a man commandeered a group of men and women into a queue. They were around thirty people waiting for the bus and had already dutifully formed a line along the curb. He insisted that the line be perpendicular to the road, rather than parallel to it. The looks on the commuters' faces said it all: I am tired. This is insane. Why don't you leave us alone? And yet, they obeyed. Begrudgingly, without protest. North Korea had its share of such bullies, those who thrived on exerting control, even or especially when it served no useful purpose. It reminded me of my military service in France, where you could always count on some low-ranking guy to enforce discipline just for the sake of it.

Even in the extremely constrained society of the DPRK, coercion can only go so far. Motivation counts. And this is where the value of duty comes into play. I was once surprised by a remark from a group of nurses that exemplified this principle. I had commended them for their diligent efforts in caring for children at a nursery, 'You are working hard for these children,' I said. One of the staff responded to me with a note of surprise. 'Working hard? It is our duty,' she replied. Her response could seem on the face of it routine and utterly insincere. That evening at the Random Access Club, I mentioned our visit to friends. Someone nodded. 'Yes, that is their usual response. North Koreans genuinely believe it's their duty to do their best.' Another commented. 'Given the conditions of work, the scarcity and hardness of the system, maybe this is submission. But it can also be a cover for perseverance, kind of a stubborn survival. They do what they can. That is why the system still works. But leaders beware: duty is a double-edged sword; it can just as easily turn against its original master.'

* * *

Throughout my assignment to North Korea, when I described 'engagement' I often faced the valid criticism that we were not doing enough to promote human rights. I acknowledged this shortcoming and sought ways to address it, albeit in a restrained manner. Humanitarian agencies traditionally avoid mixing politics with aid, and raising human rights issues in North Korea could prove particularly risky – representatives of various organizations had been, in the past, declared *persona non grata* (undesirable) for doing so. Moreover, at the time, the UN Secretary-General did not explicitly include human rights into the Resident Coordinator's mandate.

It was hard to imagine negotiating a rights-based approach in a place that did not possess the vocabulary, let alone the will, to conceive of a society where individual freedom can be freely expressed. But we had to try, and my idea was to use our relationships with the government and gradually push back against specific restrictions within our existing projects. Though I knew the DPRK faced global criticism for its military nuclear development, I also saw its desire for acceptance as a full member of the international community, exemplified by its pursuit of UN membership.

At the UN, one entry point could be found from the international human rights conventions that North Korea did sign. These included the Convention on the Rights of Persons with Disabilities (CRPD), the Convention on the Rights of the Child, and the Convention on the

Elimination of All Forms of Discrimination Against Women (CEDAW). UNICEF stood at the forefront of efforts to promote the rights of children and women. UNFPA, WHO and UNICEF tried to promote the establishment of a comprehensive health monitoring system for women. But the Government met our attempts at engagement around CEDAW with a flat dismissal: 'North Korea achieved gender equality long ago!' This was more than disappointing; it was so plainly ridiculous that it was hard to see a way to engage the government.

Disability rights offered another potential entry point. The Belgium branch of Handicap International had established a powerful practice around disability in North Korea. They worked closely with the Korean Federation of People with Disability (KFPD) and did excellent work over the years. They helped us at the UN, notably UNICEF, UNFPA, and WHO, develop a training curriculum for national health professionals, introduce new health and rehabilitation protocols for people with disabilities, and explained to others benefits of the CRPD. When the national Census was being prepared, the National Federation supported the UN and Switzerland's proposal to add eight questions on disability, an action that strengthened the national census.

But it was tough going. Our efforts remained very limited in scope and impact. When UN programming documents called for providing assistance to 'the most vulnerable people, groups, and regions of the country', we knew we had no means of reaching people without homes, the street children or those held in detention centres and prison labour camps. Nor did the UN provide election monitoring, a common mandate in other countries. The most we could do was find ways to raise human rights issues as a regular aspect of our dialogue and work process, and when possible, establish a foothold. Our efforts aimed to influence key actors, talk about and normalize the values of rights-based programming, and bring a few people and policies a little closer to international standards.

* * *

These minor successes hardly compensated what I felt was my agency's lack of courage in supporting those North Koreans who, inside the system, tried to advance an agenda towards opening. One of my objectives was to help the DPRK join the concert of nations that report on the Millennium Development Goals or MDGs. In the year 2000, somewhat miraculously, not one of the five permanent members of the UN Security Council was involved in a conflict and a majority of nations seemed united and at peace. That year, UN Secretary General Kofi Annan launched a framework for the world to work collaboratively. He proposed targets he called the Millennium Development Goals (MDGs) and made them measurable. They aimed at reducing poverty, hunger, disease, illiteracy, environmental degradation, and discrimination against women, with a target date of 2015. Every single nation – including the DPRK – committed to these goals in a global consensus not likely to be equalled again. In the DPRK, each UN Agency actively supported the DPRK Government in their efforts to meet their targets and monitored improvement.

When I arrived, however, the country had not yet started to report on their progress with meeting the MDGs. But the Government readily agreed to try. I knew it would be a rocky adventure. Would the DPRK report honestly on objectives which, almost by definition had no vocabulary and were not soon attainable? Could North Korea actually admit to shortcomings?

This is exactly what MFA and Central Bureau of Statistics officers tried to achieve, with the UN's support. The report came out in June 2011. Of course, the report was beset with excuses like, '*In successive years, however, the DPRK was faced with major difficulties throughout the overall economy as well as with respect to the people's living standards owing to the external economic pressure and blockade, flood damage for successive years from the mid-1990s and the disruption of the trade links with the former socialist countries*.' There wasn't a word on the regime's interdiction of private liberties, markets and personal initiatives. And the report contained excessive, plainly implausible statements. The North Korean government in all its bravado claimed near-perfect literacy, universal employment without mention of forced labour and without discussing chronic malnutrition.

Yet, as I watched the report-making process, I saw how hard MFA staff and the statistics office pushed boundaries, trying to inject slivers of honesty into an otherwise rigid and often misleading system. For once, the report (and by extension North Korea) openly admitted to a few of its failures: a decayed water supply, the lack of proper sanitation, the presence of unsupported disabled people in society. Not much, but a beginning.

Very quickly, almost reflexively, UNDP rejected the report and refused to publish it. I was disappointed in my own agency's managers and in my inability to convince them otherwise. I read the comments from analysts who sat in New York and in regional headquarters, far from the daily reality of working in an autocratic regime. Had I been too naive to think the admittedly flawed report constituted progress and was, consequently, worth promoting? Did I miscalculate, believing that small cracks in the DPRK's propaganda machine could lead to real change?

But mostly I felt for the unknown but committed MFA and Statistics Officer when I informed him or her that the mighty UN would not publish their report. That officer was our creation, our Trojan horse, our agent of change. He or she knew it. And sometimes paid the price for it, living under suspicion, an individual 'tainted' by his training and frequent contacts with the outside. Why then couldn't UNDP own up to its responsibility? I thought of the risks that he took, the battles that he fought inside a system that did not tolerate dissent. He risked a lot more than any of us. And when the time came for the international community to say, 'We see what you're trying to do – let's build on it,' we instead turned away. In the end, in a somewhat dignified response, I thought, the North Korean Government chose to spend their own money and published the report by themselves.

I felt that the UN had missed a chance. We failed not just the courageous individuals inside the regime who tried their best to use facts, figures and information to move an agenda, we also made things more difficult for the future. Opportunities for engagement in North Korea are rare, fragile things. The door that I thought I'd help crack open, was shut once more.

However disappointed I felt with myself and my organization, I had enough experience by then to know that we'd get another chance. Progress would take time and there would be setbacks just as major as this one. I was about to experience yet another instance when hope for change takes time to materialize.

Part III

Exit and Reflection

Chapter 13

Transition without Change

Passing of Kim Jong Il – The Funeral – International reactions – Hopes for reforms – Getting ready to leave DPRK – Train from Beijing

'While North Korea's theoretical collapse, often equated with regime change, has been anticipated at least three times since the end of the Cold War – following the death of Kim Il Sung, the North Korean famine in the mid to late 1990s, and the ascension of Kim Jong Un in 2012 – it has yet to materialize. Moreover, the contemporary debate surrounding the regime's ending increasingly emphasizes that any crisis is more likely to stem from challenges to Kim Jong Un's leadership, rather than from a rapid regime change. [. . .] For leadership collapse to occur, factors such as viable alternatives to Kim's regime and credible assurances of security and stability outside North Korea would be required; however, in the absence of such conditions, elites are more likely to support the regime as a survival strategy, thereby opting for a "shared fate".'[1]

* * *

When Kim Jong Il died on Monday, 17 December 2011, the announcement came not from within North Korea, but through a crack in its walls – the outside world knew before the people inside. I remember that morning clearly: the thin winter light, the silence of the city, the way the news on my internet radio unsettled the air before anything had officially changed. In Pyongyang, the streets remained orderly, as always, but something invisible had shifted. It was as though the country itself was holding its breath.

The news took me by surprise. No one in our community had any inkling of his imminent death prior to the announcement, even though the Leader's ill health was being commented upon in the foreign press.

I was uncertain about how this would affect our work, safety, and that of our North Korean staff. When they arrived that morning, they seemed unaware of the news. But the country was not about to enter chaos. The regime's meticulous management of information meant they were preparing the people before making it official. I felt that Kim likely died days ago, but they ensured everyone was in their work units before announcing it. Despite functioning as usual, there was fear – of people's reaction, foreign interference and uncertainty. I alerted our local Security Management Team and the New York office. In North Korea, you brace for storms before they appear.

After hearing the news, the North Korean staff had red-rimmed eyes from crying. I spoke to Kim Ri Sol, a senior colleague.

'It makes me happy that our dear *Changgunnim* is free from suffering for us,' Kim said, referring to the departed Leader as 'General'.

'In what way did he suffer?' I asked.

'He died of exhaustion worrying and working for the people,' Kim explained with sincere emotion. I reflected on Kim's words: *working to death for the people*. Wasn't it what the Leader instructed his own people?

'We are so happy that he is in a better place.'

'What place is that?'

Kim looked at me, unsure what to say next. I pressed on, gently. 'Is he going to Paradise?'

Kim hesitated. I could tell that he had no religious education at all. Yet, he had heard about Western religions, so he knew some of it. I wanted to understand how they processed death.

'I don't know what that is.'

'Mr Kim, some people, where I come from, believe that you go back to eternal life in a place called Paradise.'

'No. Only Kim Il Sung, the Father of our Nation, is immortal.'

Kim looked as though he was struggling with that question. His red-rimmed eyes darted, his shoulders hunched and tense, revealing more than just grief. He looked lost and scared, like anyone does when a catastrophe might happen, unsure of where to go or what to do next. '*One single man impacted the lives of 25 million people*,' I thought. '*Kim's rule dictated life or death for each person in North Korea, a frightening but known danger. Now, the next threat is unknown, which is even more terrifying*.'

What followed was a season of deep quiet and elaborate mourning. A few days later, the entire office attended a flower-laying ceremony on Kim Il Sung Square. We travelled in cars and vans. It was cold. We entered the plaza from the MFA side and proceeded to the front of the rows of people. Thousands stood in silence. I observed the palace where, a year earlier, a military parade had been held and Kim Jong Il was seen standing on the balcony. Pyongyang was quieter than usual, with no loudspeakers or commands – only silence.

And then I heard the sound, like the whisper of billions of tiny drops of water. A ripple of grief. I turned to look behind me. Thousands of men and women dressed in black sniffled between quiet sobs and whimpers. My skin prickled. *This is too much.* It was an unnatural, oppressive grief, like a tidal wave that would not be denied. I wanted to leave. My mind whirled as we waited. Our Korean colleagues set up the wreath on its triangular support, and the ripple of sobbing eventually reached us. Our colleagues began to whimper. Some openly wept. The sound was growing, pressing against us like a slow-moving tide.

And then – A tingling around my eyes. *Dammit. No. I won't cry.* I clenched my jaw, forcing my body to obey. I would not cry. But the weight of it all – *the mass hysteria, the sheer scale of it* – was undeniable. Thinking back to this moment, I dared anyone to stand on that plaza and not feel it pressing into them.

Three days later, we briefly met young Kim Jong Un at the viewing of his father's body. Kumsusan Palace, already housing Kim Il Sung's body since 1994, would now also hold Kim Jong Il. Kim Jong Un was guarded but curious as Carolyn and I approached him among the Diplomatic

Figure 13.1 Carolyn and Jerome at the wake of Kim Jong Il. Photo by Korean Central News Agency.

Corps members. I had previously encountered Kim and his sister, Kim Yo Jong, at a museum visit with expatriate friends, where he showed similar interest in our diverse group. The Russian diplomat next to me bowed from his waist down; I lowered my head a little; Carolyn stood, staring ahead.

* * *

On the day of the funeral, to which I was to go alone, the weather reflected the sombre event: bitter cold, slippery ice, snowy sky. At 8 am in the morning, Mr Pak and I slowly inserted our Audi into a funeral procession, UN flag showing. We snaked our way between masses of population pressing themselves on both sides of the road, so close that their faces, tight and inexpressive, beaten by wind and snow, could touch the car's windows. The crowd undulated and heaved like one massive living being. Everyone, even the old, the sick, the disabled stood outside along the road. I once saw one person crying loudly, and that set off the group around him. At some point, someone decided to throw his coat on the road to keep the snow from covering it. Many persons followed his example, exposing themselves to the bitter cold. More than one person looked annoyed with having to do that. I could not tell for certain whether the grief was genuine or they felt they had to. Our convoy stretched and stretched amid convulsed, frigid bodies and faces, then stopped and waited, then resumed slowly. The day was going to be long.

I stepped out of the car by the gates of Kumsusan Memorial Palace, the gigantic vault for Kim Il Sung, where the son's embalmed body would be permanently displayed in the same manner as his father. I had visited the Mausoleum, mixing Communist iconography with Christian mystic flamboyance. Marble arched columns lined the halls, bronze-like busts of people grieving for the Father of the Nation. His white marble statue bathed in artificial light and radiance next to huge rooms filled with awards, medals and photographs given to Kim in his lifetime by foreign countries, universities, and friendship associations from around the world and from world leaders. In the spiralling snow, ushers pressed us along, shouting '*Pali, Pali!*' (Hurry!), herding us to an elevated terrace outside the Palace facing the gate and a park, then running back to shepherd more guests to our spot.

We stood in the cold for hours, overlooking the park, the Mausoleum to our back. At one point I saw Antonio Inoki, the Japanese wrestler and actor and friend of Kim Jong Il. With his 6 ft 3 in (1.91 m) and 224 lb (102 kg), he towered over everyone. Eventually I got so cold, I could no longer feel my toes. The snow had stopped when the funeral procession finally arrived. I counted four 1964 Black Lincoln Continental Limousines (the first one carried the coffin), forty Mercedes E Series, all black, and forty Volkswagen Passat, all white. As sombre music played, the procession walked past us. Kim Jong Un walked along the Lincoln, holding its rear-view mirror. The procession entered the Mausoleum, and it was over. Everyone dashed madly to their cars, exhausted and frozen.

* * *

Kim Jong Il's death prompted pundits around the world to predict fundamental change to the DPRK. After all, they wrote, Kim Jong Un was young, Swiss-educated – surely, he would bring reform. From my vantage point, I wasn't convinced. The system seemed built to sustain itself, not to change. The first public event under the young leader reinforced that belief. On Kim Il Sung Square, we watched as one representative from each part of the regime – Government, Party elements such as the Korean Democratic Women's Union, the military and so on – took turns reading prepared statements pledging allegiance to the new Leader. The script was identical – only the organization's name changed. As far as I could see, the machine continued, uninterrupted.

Some experts outside of the country did warn against undue expectations for change. The Korea Times published an article describing Kim Jong Un's 'three protective circles' – the ruling family, the Korean Workers' Party, and the Korean People's Army. The message was clear: the country was not teetering on the brink of transformation. It was tightening its grip. The country's political system was completely unified, the authors concluded, around the new face of North Korea.[2]

At that point however, we noticed small signs that something new was afoot. A few words here and there – more measured, less harsh. Murmurs of modest changes, trial reforms, gestures of openness. We noticed Kim Jong Un's twenty-minute speech, broadcast live, in a normal tone of voice; the time when he expressed 'gratitude to foreign friends, who are extending their positive support to the just cause of our people'; or when I heard him say that the people should not have to 'tighten their belts' any longer. I noticed Kim's uncle Jang Song Taek at a military parade in Pyongyang in February 2012. He'd be seen toasting with guests including some foreign Ambassadors. Word spread that he had wrestled control of important offices, notably mining, from the military. Jang was regarded as a reformist, busy seeking more investments from China with whom he was said to be close.

We started to hear about small but intriguing changes in agriculture policy. Several European NGOs, returning from cooperative farms gave the news at the Friday Inter Agency Meeting: 'They're testing agricultural reforms in three counties in Ryanggang Province,' they announced. 'The size of the average cooperative farm production unit might be reduced to four or six people . . .'

'Four or six people?' I exclaimed. 'That sounds a lot like the size of the family, without calling it that.'

'And there is more,' they would continue. 'Under this experiment, each 'unit' receives 30 per cent of the target production and the state keeps 70 per cent. If the unit exceeds the target, then they get to keep the surplus.'[3] Others had heard more news of agricultural reform: 'Grain will be procured at market prices.' While others had heard: 'They are providing new seed varieties, fertilizer, weeding implements.'

And then, around that time, the Associated Press opened a bureau in Pyongyang, becoming the first international news organization with a full-time presence to cover news from North Korea in words, pictures and video. It was headed by a Korean-American and experienced journalist. That was when we allowed ourselves to wonder: could this be the beginning of something different?

Another cause for hope was a 'Food-for-Nukes' agreement between the United States and the DPRK. Leni came to me at the end of February, looking thrilled. 'North Korea and the US are entering into a deal. If the DPRK agrees to implement a moratorium on long-range missile launches, nuclear tests and nuclear activities at Yongbyon, including uranium enrichment activities,' she explained, 'the United States will release 240,000 metric tons in food aid. The food will be distributed by US NGOs and ourselves at WFP.'

This agreement, called the Leap Day Deal because it was concluded on 29 February meant a positive step towards peace and a serious boost in food aid. 240 thousand metric tons could go a long way towards covering the annual food deficit! Maybe I could allow myself to be hopeful?

In the end, the stirrings of change completely vanished. The results of the agricultural reform experiments in Ryanggang Province were not reported. Farmers were expected to receive bonuses for rice paddy, maize, wheat, and barley beyond the stated prices during 2010 and 2011. However, there was no confirmation of any changes in the pricing system or receipt of such bonuses. Instead, it was noted that sub-work teams received certain benefits for exceeding production targets, which is part of a traditional incentive system. These measures did not represent a modern incentive system or the marketing changes necessary for improving economic efficiency and increasing food production over the long term.

A few months later, all hopes of reform were brutally shut down. The failed April 2012 satellite launch torpedoed the Leap Day Deal. The December launch of Kwangmyongsong-3 Unit 2 confirmed what many had feared: the regime's strategic priority remained survival at any cost. At the end of the year, Kim Jong Un's uncle Jang Sung Taek and surviving relatives were purged and executed, including children. I had already left the country in January, but my friends told me of the chill everyone felt, internationals and Koreans alike.

I then remembered a slogan a North Korean man told me: 'In North Korea, everything is political.' Kim Jong Un had ruthlessly reminded his people to never forget this principle.

* * *

The year was concluding and my tenure in North Korea was coming to an end. The head of the International Department at the MFA, Mr Yun Tae Song, invited me to a farewell dinner. Mr Choe was present (Mr Song had departed North Korea a few months earlier for an assignment to a friendly nation – he didn't inform me of his reassignment. Choe did). I brought up the topic of reforms we had heard about, but which increasingly appeared as mere adjustments within an otherwise static system.

'These reforms will enhance the efficiency of DPRK agriculture,' he elucidated. 'They represent advancements in our Korean-style socialism.'

I attempted to counter, 'How can you integrate foreign investments and technology without steering the DPRK away from a command economy and its doctrines?'

Without much forethought, I added, 'In China and Vietnam . . .' hoping to draw a comparison. However, Yun interrupted me.

'We are not moving away from socialism. What you should understand about our country, is that we are first of all striving to survive as a society.'

'I understand that people need to trust that they will be supported to endure and prosper, and that it will happen in a fair manner,' I answered.

He put an end to that conversation: 'Our economy and society adhere to their unique path. We refer to it as: socialism of our own style.'

* * *

Carolyn and I prepared for another North Korean winter, our last one, in its numbing cold and natural beauty. I woke up one morning, unable to see through our windows. Frost had arrived, covering them on the inside, with delicate, elegant frond-like designs. During a walk on Ryongak Hill, southwest of Pyongyang, we marvelled at the delicate frost highlighting each twig on trees but noticed that it equally covered the faces and scarves of bicyclists braving the cold.

We celebrated the new year returning by overnight train from Beijing to Dandong. In the morning, on New Year's Day, we rode from Dandong (Sinuiju on the Korean side) to Pyongyang. Everything was white, frozen and beautiful under the low morning sun. Scenes of daily life slowly passed by, reminding me of old Korean paintings, with rural residents 'clad in white clothing', as my Korean-language teacher would sometime call the Korean people, referring to the past, when most Koreans wore white clothes. This would be our last entrance into North Korea.

Figure 13.2 View from the train in winter. Photo by Jerome Sauvage.

EPILOGUE

As I finish this account of my time in North Korea, six years have passed since the country sealed its borders in response to the Covid-19 pandemic. The presence of the international community – flawed, fragile, yet vital – vanished overnight and has not returned. In the silence that followed, ordinary lives have grown even more obscured, hidden behind high walls and closed borders.

I am trying to imagine what six years without international aid really means, without food assistance, childhood vaccinations or maternal healthcare. For the UN working on behalf of the international community, we've lost the vital window we once had into the country's population – and with it, the ability to report those realities to the world. Today I fear deprivation has deepened – undocumented, unmeasured, unanswered. It is certainly time for international cooperation to resume in the DPRK.

Yet if North Korea were to reopen tomorrow, I worry that international actors and organizations will not have learned from previous hard experience, and aid programmes will be subjected to the same geopolitical pressures as in the past. We risk to reflexively end up once again in the familiar 'food-versus-nukes' paradigm. As an advocate for development, I find this to be a false choice, ending in a failed strategy[1] that not only did not deter the DPRK's nuclear ambitions but consistently impeded efforts to assist the North Korean people.

The current instability and realignments on the global stage, combined with the US's retreat from its leadership role in international development, threaten to divert the international community's attention and resources away from the DPRK. As a result, the DPRK risks slipping further down the global agenda, with even less attention and priority allocated to its pressing humanitarian needs, ongoing security concerns, and persistent economic isolation. This diminished focus could manifest as reductions in humanitarian assistance, fewer diplomatic initiatives aimed at engagement or dialogue, and a weakening of international scrutiny regarding security or human rights issues within the DPRK.

I appreciate the calls for a different kind of posture towards the DPRK such as 'stable coexistence' with Pyongyang, which would emphasize risk reduction and improved relations with North Korea while maintaining deterrence[2].

If the international community can coalesce towards a posture of acknowledgement of the reality of the DPRK as a nuclear State, then perhaps we can imagine a form of engagement that would allow for a broader dialogue on human security for the North Korean people, including human development and human rights[3]. Humanitarian aid would then resume to alleviate the worst aspects of poverty; development agencies could address structural improvements in health, agriculture, energy, climate resilience; and such a dialogue could begin to build relationships, zones of cooperation, even trust.

We in the international community must also reflect on our own contradictions. Although I did witness three years of milestones in the country, I was not merely a witness. I was also an active though certainly imperfect interlocuter, my cooperation and impact limited in scope inside a much larger story.

While there is no predictable timeline for building a different future, I can only reflect on the importance of my own residency in-country for three years as critical to whatever success we had, or lessons we learned. Together, North Korean and international colleagues developed a dimension of mutual confidence through years of present and clear-eyed cooperation without facile concessions. It was a place where the space for humanitarian work was constricted but where hope and resilience persisted in small but meaningful ways.

When change does come to North Korea, it will come from the people of North Korea, hard-working and caring about their families and each other and from those who have the will and the ability to make life more bearable under the system.

Behind the geopolitics and propaganda and isolation, there remain human beings – resilient, intelligent and dignified – who continue to endure, to wait, and to hope.

APPENDIX

Anyone who seeks to complement this book with primary-source documentation may wish to look into the following documents that I referred to in the text.

DPRK Documents

MDG Progress Report June 2011.
New Year Editorial, 2010.

UN: General

Report of the US Senate Investigation into UNDP, 2008.
United Nations in DPRK Overview Funding Document, 2010.

Food in the DPRK

FAO/WFP 2010 Crop and Food Assessment.
FAO/WFP 2011 Crop and Food Assessment.

Energy in the DPRK

Potential Renewable Energy Technology Applications for Demonstration by Zharas Takenov and Tran Quang Cu, July 2011.

Report on Energy Assessment and Engineering Design in Hoechang County, 2011.

Yaksu Gasification Basic Design and Technical Specifications, 2011.

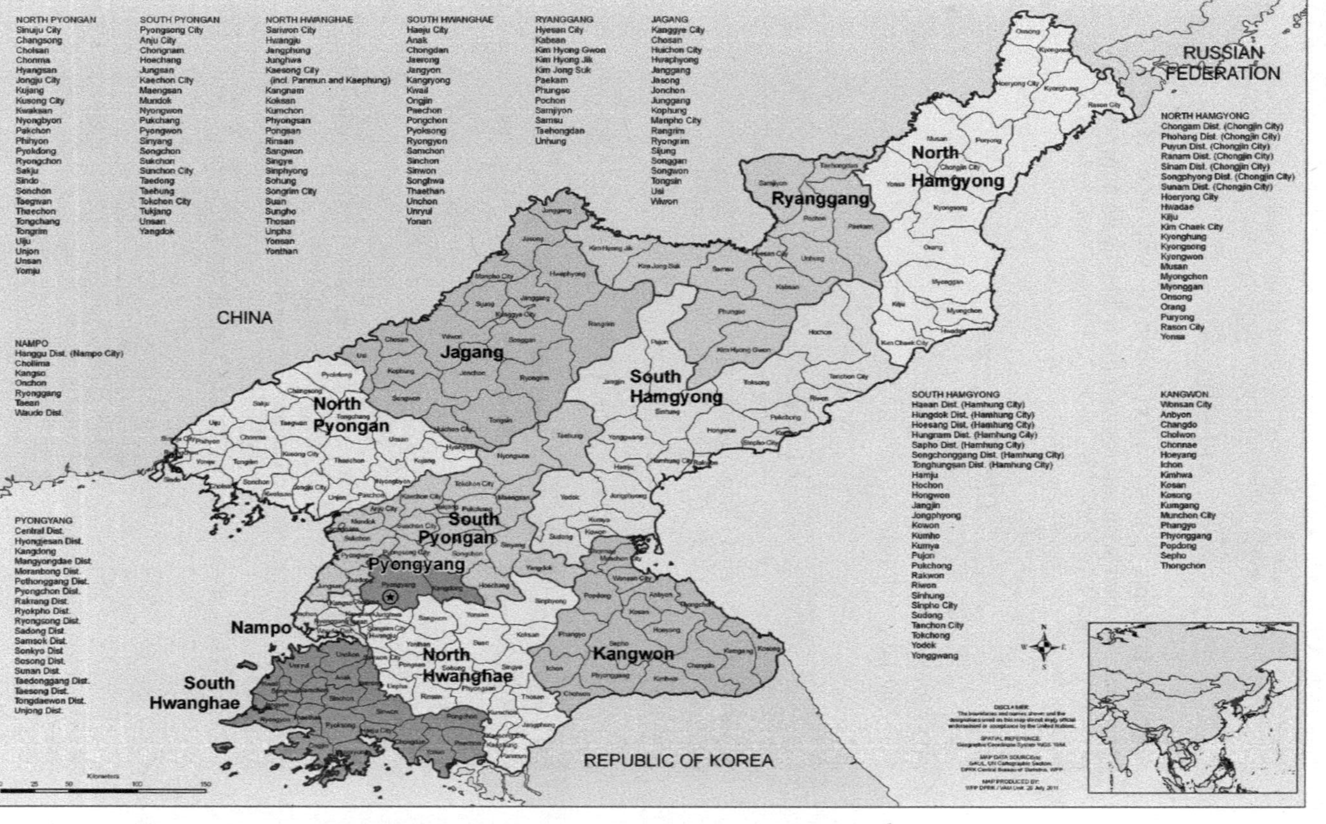

Figure A.1 Administrative map of North Korea issued by the UN in DPRK in 2011 (WORD).

NOTES

Preface

1 Nazanin Zadeh-Cummings, Karin Janz and James Banfill, with Jasmine Barrett and Ian Bennett, '(Re)Engagement with the People of the Democratic People's Republic of Korea (DPRK): Dialogue and Planning for Future Opportunity', Centre for Humanitarian Leadership, November 2023.

Chapter 1

1 See UNESCO World Heritage Sites: http://nationalatlas.ngii.go.kr/pages/page_2040.php.

Chapter 1.5

1 Fox News, 19 January 2007, https://shorturl.at/ynvuY.
2 Agreement between the Government of the DPRK and UNDP concerning assistance by the UNDP to the Government of the DPRK, signed 8 November 1979.
3 United States Senate Permanent Subcommittee on Investigations Committee on Homeland Security and Governmental Affairs, *United Nations Development Programme: A Case Study of North Korea*, 24 January 2008.
4 'Second Probe of UNDP–North Korea Scandal Set to Begin', Fox News, 7 July 2007, www.foxnews.com.
5 'Secret Legal Memo Urges UN Development Office to Rehire Whistleblower', Fox News, 12 September 2007, www.foxnews.com.
6 US Senate Panel report, *United Nations Development Programme*, p. 42.
7 External Independent Investigative Review Panel, *Confidential Report on United Nations Development Programme Activities in the Democratic People's Republic of Korea, 1999–2007*, 31 May 2008; and conversations with UNDP staff members involved in the case.
8 Members of the Panel include: Miklós Németh, Chair, former Prime Minister of Hungary (1988-1990); Chander Mohan Vasudev, Executive Director for India, Bangladesh and Sri Lanka at the World Bank; Mary Ann Wyrsch, former senior executive in the U.S. Government, most recently former Deputy Commissioner of the Immigration and Naturalization Service.

9 'Report of the UNDP Executive Board on Its Work during 2007', *Economic and Social Council Official Records*, 2007, Supplement No. 15: 'In 2002, the DPRK government used its relationship with the United Nations to execute deceptive financial transactions by moving $2.72 million of its own funds from Pyongyang to DPRK diplomatic missions abroad through a bank account intended to be used solely for UNDP activities and by referencing UNDP in the wire transfer documents' and that 'UNDP transferred UN funds to a company that . . . has ties to an entity involved in DPRK weapons activity.' US Senate Permanent Subcommittee on Investigations under the Committee on Homeland Security and Governmental Affairs.
10 Ibid.
11 'Annan Says Iraq War was "Illegal"', *New York Times*, 16 September 2004.
12 UNDP Executive Board Decision 2009/1 Proposed Measures for the Resumption of UNDP Programme Operations in the Democratic People's Republic of Korea.

Chapter 2

1 In North Korea, the Juche calendar dates years from 1912, the year of Kim Il Sung's birth (Year 1). To convert from Juche to Western years, add 1911. ('99' equates to '2010'.)
2 As John Everard wrote, 'with the failed economic measures of November 2009, the food supply dried up and some embassies found that the only edible substance on sale was chocolate', in *Only Beautiful Please: A British Diplomat in North Korea* (Stanford, CA: Stanford University Press, 2012), chapter 5, para. 18.
3 Marcus Noland, *North Korea's Failed Currency Reform*, 5 February 2010, BBC Online, Peterson Economic Institute, www.piie.com/commentary/op-eds/north-koreas-failed-currency-reform.

Chapter 3

1 Paul French, *North Korea: State of Paranoia*, Asian Arguments Series (London: Bloomsbury Publishing).
2 For a complete view of UN programmes, see UN Office for the Coordination of Humanitarian Affairs, *Overview Funding Document*, 2010.
3 The hunger strikes back an epigenetic memory for autophagy by Patricia González-Rodríguez, Jens Füllgrabe and Bertrand Joseph, *Nature*, 8 April 2023, at: www.nature.com/articles/s41418-023-01159-4.

4 UN, *Overview of Needs and Assistance Democratic People's Republic of Korea*, December 2010.
5 'North Korea Refuses to Abandon Nukes', CNN, 21 February 2010, 10.41 pm. EST

Chapter 4

1 The KPA encompasses the combined military forces of the DPRK and the armed wing of the WPK. It consists of five branches: ground forces, navy, air force, strategic force (artillery and missiles) and special operations forces.
2 Patrick McEachern suggests that Kim Jong Il's regime became less centralized than his father's and that North Korean politics comprise the interaction of the military, party and cabinet with 'oversight' by the security apparatus. These semi-autonomous groups have opportunity and cause to interact in the policy formation and execution process and enjoy limited autonomy with Kim and his inner circle of advisers holding final authority. For an analysis on how the state's political institutions debate policy and inform and execute strategic-level decisions, read Patrick McEachern, *Inside the Red Box: North Korea's Post-totalitarian Politics* (New York: Columbia University Press, 2010).
3 French, *North Korea*.
4 Martin Fackler, 'A Capitalist Enclave in North Korea Survives', *New York Times*, 6 July 2010.
5 Monthly Note to the Emergency Relief Coordinator, UNCT DPRK, 23 April–31 May 2010.
6 For a word on a more recent impact of sanctions on NGOs working in the DPRK, see American Friends Service Committee, *Engaging North Korea*, 2016; and Hazel Smith, 'The Impact of Sanctions on Humanitarian Assistance to the DPRK', Open Nuclear Network, 1 August 2024, https://shorturl.at/wfzwY.
7 On cyber criminality by the DPRK, see Jean H. Lee and Geoff White, *The Lazarus Heist*, BBC Podcast, 10 September 2025.
8 On sanctions and security in North-East Asia, see John Delury, Morton Halperin, Peter Hayes, Chung-In Moon, Leon Sigal and Tom Pickering, 'Revisiting the Comprehensive Security Roadmap to Reduce the Risk of War on the Korean Peninsula', NAPSNET, Special Report, 19 April 2024.

Chapter 5

1 'Table 1: Energy Consumption per Capita in Rural Households, DPR Korea', in 'Sustainable Rural Energy Development', project document, p. 7.

2 David von Hippel and Peter Hayes, *Energy Insecurity in the DPRK: Linkages to Regional Energy Security and the Nuclear Weapons Issue*, Nautilus Institute for Security and Sustainability, 2018.

3 See CBS/UNDP, *Energy Consumption Survey 2005*; UNDP, *Report on Energy Assessment Survey and Engineering Design for More Efficient and Effective Electricity Production in Hoechang Hydro-Power Stations*, 2010.

4 UNIDO, *Report on Energy Assessment Survey and Engineering Design for More Efficient and Effective Electricity Production in Hoechang Hydro-Power Stations*, 2010.

5 See 'Directive on Food Situation – Extract Item No. 2: "To Each Ministry of Industries, Do the Best You Can to Prevent Workers Suffering from Hunger"', 26 May 2010. A directive asking to take measures to ensure livelihood for labourers at each agency and enterprise was issued to each ministry, including the Ministry of Light Industry. The main message was to inform that the government is unable to provide food distribution and ask them to revive the factories so that they can handle the food problem on their own for their workers. It said that since the workers' livelihood is in a dire condition, do the best you can to prevent workers from suffering from hunger. The directive also urged to help labourers who are unable to come to work due to starvation. Source: Research Institute For North Korean Society, 'Good Friends', No. 340, June 2010.

Chapter 6

1 French, *North Korea*.

2 Aidan Foster-Carter, 'Seoul's Secret Success', Nautilus Institute for Security and Sustainable Development, 21 November 2003.

3 Daniel Goodkind, Loraine West and Peter Johnson, 'A Reassessment of Mortality in North Korea, 1993–2008'Population Division, US Census Bureau, paper to be presented at the annual meeting of the Population Association of America, Washington, DC, 31 March–2 April 2011).

4 The US Census Bureau pointed out in a 2011 paper presented by Goodkind, West and Johnson, ibid., that: 'Such improved reporting would be consistent with the greater technical involvement of the United Nations in the latter census . . . Once reporting anomalies are corrected for, North Korea's censuses suggest a consistent and plausible picture of demographic change' (4).

5 Barbara Demick, *Nothing to Envy: Ordinary Lives in North Korea* (New York, NY: Spiegel and Grau, 2009).

6 Sonia Ryang (ed.), *North Korea: Toward a Better Understanding*, New Asian Anthropology (Lexington, MD: Rowan and Littlefield, 2009).

7 Luisa Engracia, Chief Technical Advisor for 2008 DPRK Census, '2008 Census of Population DPR Korea', 2010.

8 French, *North Korea*.

Chapter 7

1 Report of the Commission of Inquiry on Human Rights in the Democratic People's Republic of Korea, Human Rights Council, 7 February 2014.
2 FAO/WFP Crop and Food Security Assessment Mission to the Democratic People's Republic of Korea, 16 November 2010, p. 21.
3 CFSAM 2011 Final Report: 'This was the first CFSAM where members were permitted to visit daily markets in addition to farmers' markets, and state shops. Although, the mission was able to directly observe PDS distribution in only one Centre, its members did visit (PDC) and county warehouses.'
4 Overview Funding Document, UN DPRK, December 2010, p. 35.
5 Bryan Reynolds Ryan, *The Cleanest Race: How North Koreans See Themselves and Why It Matters* (Brooklyn, NY: Melville House Publishing, 2010).
6 Ryang (ed.), *North Korea.*
7 FAO/WFP CFSAM 2010, p. 23.
8 John Everard, 'The Markets of Pyongyang', *KEI Academic Paper Series*, 6, no. 1a (January 2011).
9 'North Korea Progress at a Snail's Pace', *The Economist*, 9 October 2003.
10 Peterson Institute for International Economics, Policy Brief, Number PB10-1, January 2010, p. 6.
11 FAO/WFP Crop And Food Security Assessment Mission to the Democratic People's Republic of Korea 11/2011, p. 26.
12 DPRK military is not included in these numbers, having their own sources of grain.

Chapter 8

1 Report on basic design and equipment technical specifications of 100 kw rice husk gasification power plant in Yaksu cooperative farm, full advantage company limited, Thailand, 17 September 2011.

Chapter 9

1 Barbara Demick, *Nothing to Envy: Ordinary Lives in North Korea* (New York, NY: Spiegel and Grau, 2009).
2 NK Economy Watch, 'UNDP Wind Power Project', 24 September 2012, www.nkeconwatch.com/2012/09/24/undp-wind-power-project.
3 For one of the best descriptions of everyday life for expatriates, see Everard, *Only Beautiful Please.*

Chapter 10

1 UNFPA Country Programme Evaluation, 2015.

Chapter 11

1 Sunghee Kim, *Authority and Emotions: Kim Jong Il and Religious Imagination in North Korean Literature*, East Asian Languages and Civilizations (Cambridge, MA: Harvard University, 2017), p. 8.
2 Office of the Resident Coordinator, 'DPRK: Heavy Rain Damage: Situation Report #2', 27 July 2011.
3 FAO WFP, 'Crop and Food Assessment, DPRK', 2011.
4 Office of the Resident Coordinator, 'DPRK Floods: Situation Report #3', 27 September 2010.
5 FAO WFP, 'Crop and Food Assessment, DPRK', p. 24.

Chapter 12

1 Kim, *Authority and Emotions*, p. 172.

Chapter 13

1 Won Gon Park, *Will North Korea Collapse?*, East Asia Institute, Center for North Korea Studies, Ewha Women's University, Seoul, March 2025.
2 John Delury and Chung-in Moon, 'The Death of Kim Jong Il: Now What?', *Korea Times*, 20 December 2011.
3 '6.28 Policy Goes Live in 3 Yangkang Counties', *Daily NK*, 20 July 2012.

Epilogue

1 Rachel Minyoung Lee and Jenny Town, *Move Past the Nuclear Impasse on the Korean Peninsula*, Stimmson Center, November 2024.
2 Frank Aum and Ankit Panda, *Pursuing Stable Coexistence: A Reorientation of US Policy toward North Korea*, Carnegie Endowment, 6 May 2025.
3 'A New Security Strategy Centred around the North Korean People: A Resilient Security Framework for the Korean Peninsula', *HanVoice*, March 2024.

BIBLIOGRAPHY

The literature on the DPRK is essential for whoever wants to understand a little of this country. It has helped me a lot during and after my stay. I have based this book mostly on my own experiences, but have referred to some of the literature on the DPRK.

I hope this Bibliography will serve not only to lead those who wish to examine my references to the right place, but also to help those who wish to read more about the country. I have not here listed the various scholarly articles to which I have also referred, which are referenced in the endnotes.

These books guided me in my understanding of the DPRK.

Abrahamian, Andray. *Being in North Korea*. Stanford, CA: Stanford University Press, 2020.

A first person account that combines academic rigour with excellent, easy to read writing.

Becker, Jasper. *Rogue Regime: Kim Jong Il and the Looming Threat of North Korea*. Oxford: Oxford University Press, 2005.

Demick, Barbara. *Nothing to Envy: Ordinary Lives in North Korea*. New York, NY: Spiegel & Grau, 2009.

A sobering account of the hardships of North Korea based on extensive refugee interviews.

Everard, John. *Only Beautiful Please: A British Diplomat in North Korea*. Stanford, CA: Stanford University Press, 2012.

Very informative, totally relevant and easy to read.

Flake, L. Gordon, and Scott Snyder, eds. *Paved with Good Intentions: The NGO Experience in North Korea*. Westport, CT: Praeger, 2003.

Describes the years when international cooperation began in the DPRK.

French, Paul. *North Korea: State of Paranoia*, Asian Arguments Series. London: Bloomsbury Publishing, 2015.

Published shortly after I left the country. Still the most current, complete source on DPRK today.

Haggard, Stephan, and Marcus Noland. *Witness to Transformation: Refugee Insights into North Korea*. Washington, DC: Peterson Institute For International Economics, 2011.

This book came out during my stay in North Korea. I was having an unspoken but ongoing dialogue with the authors. It supported me throughout.

Harrold, Michael. *Comrades and Strangers*. Hoboken, NJ: John Wiley & Sons, 2004.

An account of life as a foreign expert in the self-assured DPRK before the economic crises of the 1990s.

Hassig, Ralph C., and Kong Dan Oh. *The Hidden People of North Korea: Everyday Life in the Hermit Kingdom*. Lanham, MD: Rowman & Littlefield Publishers, 2009.

Everyday life in the DPRK based on refugee testimonies.

Hoare, James, and Susan Pares. *North Korea in the 21st Century: An Interpretive Guide*. Folkestone: Global Oriental, 2005.

An account of the politics of and life in the DPRK based partly on the authors' experiences while setting up the British Embassy there.

Lankov, Andrei. *The Real North Korea: Life and Politics in the Failed Stalinist Utopia*. Oxford: Oxford University Press, 2014.

A deep insight.

Martin, Bradley. *Under the Loving Care of the Fatherly Leader: North Korea and the Kim Dynasty*. New York, NY: Thomas Dunne Books, 2004.

Essential reading that hasn't gained a wrinkle.

McEachern, Patrick. *Inside the Red Box: North Korea's Post-totalitarian Politics*. New York, NY: Columbia University Press, 2010.

An important book that helped me understand who I was dealing with.

Myers, B. R. *The Cleanest Race: How North Koreans See Themselves and Why It Matters*. Brooklyn, NY: Melville House, 2010.

Another book published during my stay. An illuminating analysis of the nationalism that pervades the DPRK's political thought and propaganda.

Ryang, Sonia, ed. *North Korea: Toward a Better Understanding*, New Asian Anthropology. Lexington, MD: Rowan and Littlefield, 2009.

The author proposes a new way to look at the DPRK.

Smith, Hazel. *Hungry for Peace: International Security, Humanitarian Assistance, and Social Change in North Korea*. Washington, DC: United States Institute for Peace Press, 2005.

The impact of famine on North Korea and how we deal with it.

Snyder, Scott. *China's Rise and the Two Koreas: Politics, Economics, Security*. Boulder, CO: Lynne Rienner Publishers, 2009.

China's relationship with North (and South) Korea.

Zadeh-Cummings, Nazanin, Karin Janz and James Banfill, with Jasmine Barrett and Ian Bennett, '(Re)Engagement with the People of the Democratic People's Republic of Korea (DPRK): Dialogue and Planning for Future Opportunity', Centre for Humanitarian Leadership, November 2023.

Paper published by North Korea experts reflecting on three decades of international engagement with the DPRK, aiming to guide future efforts once the country reopens.

Expected to be published in 2026: Miss Kathi: Saving Lives In North Korea, By Kathi Zellweger And Mike Chinoy, Post Hill Press.
The story of Kathi Zellweger's remarkable work in North Korea is comprehensive, practical and offers invaluable insights for anyone interested in that country.

INDEX